Includes a 6-Session Practice Guide for Individuals and Teams

WHY MOVE MY CHEESE?

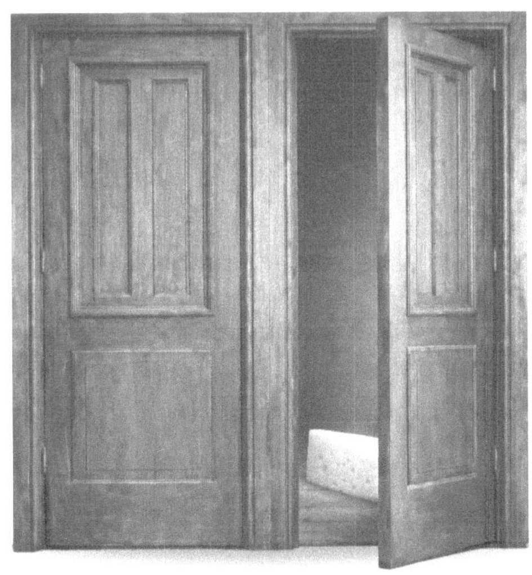

HOW TO OWN YOUR DECISIONS, TELL THE TRUTH ABOUT YOUR "WHY" AND STOP DISAPPEARING IN SEASONS OF CHANGE

DR. LAIDE R. ALEXANDER

AUTHOR OF *THE UNFINISHED LEADER*

ISBNs: 979-8-9959946-4-0 (special edition)
979-8-9959946-0-2 (mass market hardcover)
979-8-9959946-7-1 (paperback)

For more about Dr. Alexander please visit

www.accexxinsight.com

and

www.thetplat.com

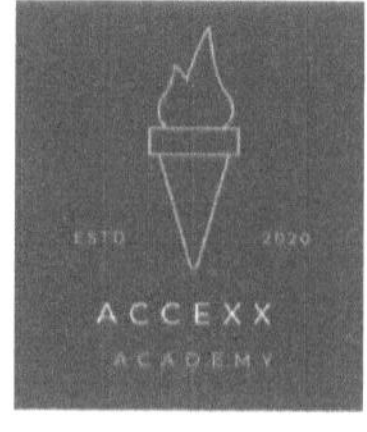

Contents

ACKNOWLEDGMENTS

This book was born in rooms where people were tired of feeling like life was always happening to them. To everyone who has ever sat across from me and said, "I don't know how I ended up here," thank you for trusting me with your stories and your questions. You taught me that we don't just survive change, we participate in it.

I want to honor Spencer Johnson, M.D., whose classic book *Who Moved My Cheese?* Gave so many of us a simple, memorable way to talk about change. His work sparked my own curiosity and became one of the inspirations behind this book. *Why Move My Cheese?* Stands on the shoulders of that earlier conversation and offers a different angle: not only who or what moves our cheese, but why we sometimes choose to move it ourselves.

To the communities I serve through the *Why Move My Cheese* conference: you are the reason this book exists. Your courage to tell the truth about your lives, your work, your faith, and your families gave me language for what it means to move your own cheese on purpose.

I am deeply grateful to the leaders, colleagues, and friends who modeled agency and accountability when it would have been easier to blame or disappear. You showed me what grown-up change looks like.

To my family, whose own moves have shaped every page, thank you for your patience, your love, and your honest feedback when my words did not yet match my life.

And finally, to every reader holding this book in a season of transition: thank you for being willing to ask not just, "Who moved my cheese?" but "Why am I moving mine?" I pray these pages help you move with more clarity, courage, and care.

To Dr. Debbie McNair, President of Draped in Praise Publishing, who first embarked on this journey with me; to Victoria McNair, whose creativity shaped the initial cover designs; and to Ms. Robin Surface, President of Fideli Publishing Inc., for her invaluable support in bringing this project to completion—thank you for believing in this message and stewarding it with such care.

Above all, I thank God for the grace, wisdom, and strength that carried me through every season that shaped this book.

Let the Conversation Begin...

INTRODUCTION

From *"Who Moved My Cheese?"* to *"Why Move My Cheese?"*

There is a question that has followed many of us through layoffs, breakups, church splits, policy changes, pandemics, and quiet personal disappointments:

Who moved my cheese?

Who changed the rules? Who took away what I depended on? Who made this decision without me? It's an honest question. It names the shock of waking up one day to find that what you counted on- a job, a role, a relationship, a ministry, a sense of identity—is no longer where you left it. ***Sometimes, that really is what happens.***

People make choices you didn't vote for. Economies shift. Leaders resign. Illness comes. Children grow up. Institutions change direction. In those moments, your cheese gets moved, and you have little or no say. This book does not deny that reality. But there is another truth we don't always name. ***Some of the most important moves in your life are the ones you make yourself.***

You leave the job. You step back from the ministry. You move to a new city. You end the relationship. You change how you show up as a parent, a partner, a leader. ***You move your own cheese.*** And when you do, another question waits: ***Why did I move my cheese?***

In Conversation With Who Moved My Cheese?

Before we go further, I want to honor the book that gave so many of us this language. In his classic parable, ***Who Moved My Cheese?*** Spencer Johnson, M.D., uses a simple story about a maze, some cheese, and a few characters to help people think about change. His book invited millions of readers to notice how they respond when life shifts—when the **"*cheese*"** they depend on is suddenly gone.

I am one of those readers.

Johnson's work sparked my curiosity and helped me talk with leaders and communities about change in a clear, memorable way. ***Why Move My Cheese?*** is not a retelling of his story. We will not follow his characters through the maze or repeat his parable. Instead, this book stands in conversation with his central question. **Where *Who Moved My Cheese?*** focuses on change that happens to us and how we adapt, ***Why Move My Cheese?*** focuses on the changes we initiate—and the deeper reasons behind them. It asks not only, "Who or what moved my cheese?" but also, "When am I the one moving it, and why?" This book is my way of extending that conversation into the very human territory of agency, accountability, and honest self-reflection.

From Blame to Agency

Over years of working with humans—not mice or cartoon characters, but real people with histories, trauma, faith, families, and bills, I noticed a gap. We were very good at talking about changes that have happened to us. We were less practiced at talking about change we choose—and the real reasons behind it. We could say, "My company restructured," but not, "I've been shrinking myself at work for years, and I'm finally done." We could say, "The church isn't what it used to be," but not, "I have outgrown some beliefs, and I'm scared to say that out loud." We could say, "They don't appreciate me," but not, "I keep agreeing to what I resent, and I'm the only one who can stop that." It is easier to ask, **"*Who moved my cheese?*"** than to admit, "I moved my cheese—and I need to tell the truth about why."

Why This Book, Why Now

I wrote *Why Move My Cheese?* because I kept meeting people in transition who felt both powerless and guilty. They were: *On the edge of a big decision* or *living with the consequences of a decision they have already made.* Some were leaving jobs, churches, or relationships. Others were changing how they led, parented, or cared for themselves. Many were saying, in one form or another: *"I know something must change. I just don't know if I'm allowed to move."* Or *"I made a move, and I'm still not sure if I did it for the right reasons."* This book is for that moment. It is not a book about perfect decisions. It is a book about honest ones.

It's an invitation to:

- Recognize where life has truly moved your cheese without your consent.

- Tell the truth about where you are choosing to move it yourself.

- Name your real "why"—the mix of fear, hope, survival, and growth underneath your decisions.

- Take responsibility for the impact of your moves on your own life and on others.

In a world that is changing rapidly, we do need to adapt to shifts we did not choose. But we also need the courage to say:

- "I am not just a victim of change. I am an agent in my own life.

- I moved my cheese, and I can explain why."

What This Book Will (and Won't) Do

This is a short book. You can read it in an afternoon or over a week. It will not:

- Tell you exactly what decision to make.

- Pretend that every move is safe or simple.

- Promise that if you move bravely, everything will work out quickly.

It will:

- Help you notice where you are standing in blame, passivity, or denial.

- Offer language for the different reasons we move: to survive, to grow, to hide, or by quietly letting others decide for us.

- Give you questions and simple frameworks to clarify your next move—or to make peace with a move you've already made.

- Invite you to move with more clarity, courage, and care.

How to Use This Book

You can read this alone, with a friend, with your partner, or with a team. At the end of each chapter, you'll find a brief "Cheese Check"—a few questions to help you pause and reflect:

- Where has your cheese been moved recently?

- Where are you moving it yourself?

- What story are you telling about that move?

- What might be a truer story?

You don't have to share your answers with anyone. But if you do, you may find you're not the only one asking these questions.

A Final Word Before We Begin

If you are holding this book, you are likely in some kind of transition. Something is ending, beginning, or shifting. Something in you knows you cannot keep living, working, or leading exactly as you have been. I want you to know this at the start:

- You are not weak because you are questioning.

- You are not selfish because you want something different.

- You are not wrong for wanting to move your cheese.

You are simply human. Let's talk about what it means to move your cheese on purpose—and to be able to say, with honesty and humility:

I moved my cheese, and here's why.

CHEESE CHECK

Take a few minutes with these questions before you move into Chapter 1. You can jot your answers in the margins, in a journal, or on your phone. Where has your cheese been moved recently? Think about work, relationships, health, faith, or community.

What changed that you did not ask for?

Where are you quietly thinking about moving your own cheese?

Is there a job, role, relationship, habit, or pattern you are considering changing?

What keeps you from saying that desire out loud?

What story are you currently telling yourself about change?

"Life keeps happening to me."

"If I move, I'll disappoint people."

"I'm not allowed to want more."

"If I don't move, I'll lose myself."

Which one sounds most like you right now?

When you think about making a move, what feeling shows up first?

Fear?

Relief?

Guilt?

Excitement?

Numbness?

Where do you feel it in your body—your chest, stomach, throat?

What would it mean for you to say, "I am allowed to move my cheese"?

How does that sentence land in your spirit? Does it feel true, threatening, hopeful, or all of the above?

You don't have to fix anything yet. For now, just notice. Your honesty here will help the rest of this book do its work.

CHEESE CHECK NOTES

If blame becomes your only story,

you get stuck in the hallway of your own life.

You keep repeating "Who moves my cheese?"

But you never get to the point of:

Okay… so what am I going to do now?

Blame can explain how you got here.

Blame cannot tell you where to go from here.

Dr. Laide R. Alexander

CHAPTER ONE

When Change Happens to You

Most of us don't go looking for change. Change comes looking for us.

You are working hard, paying your bills, serving your community, caring for your family, doing the best you can with what you have. You have a rhythm. You know where the "cheese" is—the paycheck, the role, the relationship, the routine that helps you feel safe. And then something shifts:

You get the email.

You get the phone call.

You hear the announcement.

You feel the distance.

What you counted on is no longer where you left it. *You did not move your cheese. Your cheese was moved.*

The Day the Map Stops Working. Every one of us carries a kind of invisible map in our head. On that map it says:

- If I work hard and stay loyal, I'll be secure.

- If I keep the family together, I'll be okay.

- If I stay at this church, this job, this city, I'll be safe.

- If I do what "good" people do, God will protect me from the worst.

Then life does what life does. The company "restructures" and your role is "no longer needed." The marriage you've been holding together with prayer and duct tape finally splits. The church you served for years decides to go in a direction your conscience can't follow. The body you've been running on fumes says, "Ma'am, sir, we're closed." Suddenly the map in your head says, "The cheese is right here…", reality says, "No, it's not." If you've ever stood in your own kitchen, office, car, or church parking lot and thought, "I do not know where I am anymore," you've lived this moment. That's when the question rises almost on its own; ***"Who moved my cheese?"*** It's not a bad question. It's just not the last question.

The Honest Shock of Unwanted Change. Let me say this plainly: *You are not weak for being shaken when your cheese gets moved. You are human.* Unwanted change can hit like a wave:

- **Confusion** —"What just happened?"

- **Anger** —"After everything I did, this?"

- **Embarrassment** —"What are people going to think?"

- **Fear** —"How am I going to make it?"

- **Numbness** —"I feel… nothing. I'm just going through the motions."

We sometimes try to rush past this: "Stay positive." "God's got this." "On to the next." Meanwhile, a part of us is still standing in that empty spot, whispering, "Wait… but my cheese was right here." If you don't honor that part, your unspoken grief will sneak into every decision you make next—and call it "wisdom."

It's Not Just Cheese, It's a Whole Life. When your cheese gets moved, you rarely lose only one thing. You may lose:

- **Identity** —"Who am I if I'm not the one who does this?"

- **Community** —the coworkers, church members, neighbors, or friends who knew your routine.

- **Routine** —the schedule that gave your days structure.

- **Security** —the sense that tomorrow will look like today.

- **Control** —the illusion that if you just behaved, believed, or performed "right," you could avoid pain.

This is why change can feel so dramatic, even if other people think you're "overreacting." You're not just looking for new cheese. You're grieving the whole kitchen. *There is no healthy forward movement without some honest backward glance.* Grief is not a sign you're stuck in the past. Grief is how your heart catches up with your reality.

Blame: The First Story We Reach For. In the middle of loss, blame can feel like a warm blanket. *If I can figure out exactly whose fault this is, maybe I can feel a little less helpless.*

So, we reach for a story: "They used me." "The system is against people like me." "People always leave." "Church folks are fake." "God must be punishing me." "This is just my luck—nothing good lasts."

Sometimes, there really are people and systems to name. There are unfair bosses, unjust policies, broken promises, and plain cruelty. Pretending everything is fine when it's not, is not spiritual; it's denial. But here's the problem: *If blame becomes your only story, you get stuck in the hallway of your own life.* You keep repeating, ***"Who moved my cheese?"*** but you never get to, "Okay… so what am I going to do now?" Blame can explain how you got here. Blame cannot tell you where you're going.

When You Turn the Blame Inward. Some of us don't start with blaming others. We skip everyone else and go straight to ourselves.

We re-play:

- Every time we stayed when we should have left

- Every time we left when we should have stayed

- Every email we didn't send

- Every red flag we baptized as "faith"

- Every "No" we swallowed and called it "obedience"

And the inner critic goes to work:

- "You should have known better."

- "This is what you get."

- "You always mess things up."

- "If you were smarter/holier/stronger, this wouldn't have happened."

That voice is not accountability. *That voice is shame.* Accountability says, *"I see what I did, and I'm going to grow."* Shame says, *"I see what I did, and clearly, I am trash. "* One leads to honest change. The other leads to hiding, pretending, and repeating the same patterns in a different room. You can tell the truth about your part without putting yourself on trial.

Three Layers of a Hard Moment. When your cheese has been moved, there are usually three layers to the story:

What others did
Their choices, their silence, their actions, their neglect.

What you did or didn't do
Your boundaries, your patterns, your agreements, your silences.

What nobody controlled.
Illness, death, accidents, economies, timing, pandemics, life.

Healthy responsibility lives mostly in layer two. You are not responsible for everything that was done to you. You are also not a powerless extra in your own movie. Over time, good questions sound like:

- "What was truly beyond my control?"

- "Where did I abandon myself or ignore my own knowing?"

- "What did this season reveal about what I need to learn or unlearn?"

These are grown-up questions. They hurt a little, but they move you forward. They begin to shift you from only a victim of change to also an agent in your own story—even when you didn't choose how the chapter started.

You're Allowed to Be Human About This. Before we close this chapter, let's be extremely human together. You are allowed to:

- Cry in the car.

- Be mad in the shower.

- Laugh at how wild your life looks on paper.

- Miss what you had—even if it was not good for you.

- Miss who you were—even if that version of you was shrinking to fit.

You don't have to "find the lesson" five minutes after the loss. You don't have to turn your pain into a TED Talk by next Thursday. Some days, the most honest prayer you have might be: *"Lord, I did not sign up for this. Help."* And that's okay. You don't have to be impressive right now. You just have to be honest. So if all you can say today is:

"My cheese was moved.

- I did not ask for this.

- I am upset.

- And I am still here

That's enough.

Because here is the quiet miracle: you are still here. You are breathing. You are reading. You are thinking. You are, in ways you may not feel yet, already adapting. And because you are still here, there is still something you can do next. We will talk about those choices in the chapters ahead. But first, let's pause and let you tell the truth—to yourself—about the changes that have already happened to you.

Sitting in the Empty Space. There is a strange silence that comes right after your cheese is moved. The phone may still be buzzing. The kids may still be shouting. Emails may still be pouring in. But inside, there is this quiet, echoing room where your old life used to live. You walk into that room out of habit:

- You click the app you used to check every morning.

- You drive the route you don't need to take anymore.

- You reach for a ring, a badge, a keycard that is no longer yours.

- Your body remembers the way before your mind admits the after.

This is the part of change most people don't talk about. We like the before-and-after picture. We don't like the hallway. Yet the hallway is where your nervous system is trying to understand, "Are we safe? Are we going to be okay?" If you feel "stuck," it might not be that you lack faith, discipline, or willpower. It might be that your body and mind are still catching up to a story that changed without your permission. In that empty space, you may notice:

Old coping habits creeping back—overeating, overworking, over scrolling.

Old agreements resurfacing—"See, I knew this would happen."

Old vows whispering—"Next time, I won't need anybody."

If that's you, you're not broken. You're just trying to feel steady in a room where the furniture has been moved in the dark. *Or even in the light. And sometimes, on purpose.*

The Temptation to Run Back. When the pain of "no cheese here" gets loud, almost anything familiar starts to look safe. You consider going back to the job that drained you, because at least you knew the schedule. You consider calling the person who shattered your trust, because at least you weren't lonely. You consider shrinking again to fit a space that already told you, "There is no room for the real you here." We tell ourselves stories to justify the return: "Maybe it wasn't that bad." "Maybe I overreacted." "Maybe if I try harder, behave better, it will work this time." Sometimes, a return is right. Sometimes going back happens with new boundaries, new clarity, and mutual change. But sometimes, wanting to go back is not about wisdom at all. It's about your nervous system craving the predictability of an unhealthy pattern over the uncertainty of a healthy one.

Here is a hard, gentle truth: Missing the cheese is normal. Romanticizing the cage is dangerous. You can honor what you lost without making a covenant with what almost destroyed you. If you find yourself tempted to run back to "how it was" just because "what's next" feels unfamiliar, pause and ask: "Do I miss this because it was good, or because it was familiar?", "If nothing changed there, would I still be safe going back?" "Am I reaching for comfort, or for growth?" Those questions are not to shame you. They are to keep you from voluntarily walking back into a prison whose door life has already opened.

The Stories You Tell Yourself at 2 a.m. Most of us have two versions of our story: The one we tell people in daylight, and the one we tell ourselves in the dark. *In* daylight, we say, "It was time for a change." In the dark, we whisper, "What if it was my fault?"

In daylight, we say, "I'm moving forward." In the dark, we wonder, "What if there is no real 'forward' for someone like me?" Change exposes the stories underneath our slogans. Not the affirmations we post, but the hidden lines we live by:

- "I am only as valuable as my productivity."
- "If I am not needed, I will be abandoned."
- "If I speak up, I will be punished."
- "If I rest, everything will fall apart."

When the cheese is moved, these underground beliefs float to the surface. That is painful—but it is also an invitation. You cannot heal what you refuse to see. You cannot replace a lie you will not name. So before we talk about strategies and plans and goals, I want to invite you to notice the story you tell yourself at 2:00 a.m. when nobody is asking you to be strong. Write it down if you need to. Say it out loud if you can. Even if it sounds irrational, dramatic, or "too much," it is shaping how you move.

The Difference Between Change and Harm. Not every change is an attack. Not every loss is a punishment. But there are changes that are harmful, and pretending they are neutral will only keep you stuck.

There is a difference between:

- A company restructuring because of market realities, and a leader targeting you out of bias or spite.

- A relationship drifting because both people are growing in different directions, and a partner betraying trust with lies and manipulation.

- A community shifting methods to meet new needs, and a community using power to silence questions and protect bad behavior.

Why does this matter? Because how you name what happened shapes how you heal. If you call harm "just a season," you may never give yourself permission to seek safety. If you call a natural transition "total rejection," you may carry wounds into rooms where nobody actually hurt you. Sometimes, you will need help to sort this through—a counselor, a coach, a trusted friend who can say, "No, that was not okay," or, "Yes, that was painful, but it was not a personal failure." This is not about creating drama. It is about calibrating your reality so you don't drag old battles into new beginnings.

Micro-Losses: The Little Moves That Add Up. We often notice the big moves of cheese—divorce papers, pink slips, diagnosis reports. But many of us are also living through a thousand small shifts that never make an announcement:

- The friend who replies slower and slower to your messages.

- The parent who repeats the same story because their memory is fading.

- The child whose questions are now about college instead of cartoons.

- The workplace that feels a little less like "us" and a little more like "them."

These are "micro-losses"—tiny relocations of the cheese that don't feel big enough to grieve, but still leave a mark. You tell yourself, "It's not that serious," but your mind and body feel all the tiny goodbyes. If you've been feeling unusually tired, irritable, or numb, it might not be because you are "ungrateful." It might be because you are carrying more unacknowledged change than your language has caught up with. You are allowed to name the small things too: "It hurts that my friend doesn't call like before." "It stings that my body can't do what it used to." "It's strange that my role in this family is different now." Naming micro-losses doesn't make you weak. It makes you honest. And honesty is the only ground where real adaptation can grow.

A Small, Brave Practice. Before you turn the page, I want to offer you something simple—not a solution, just a practice. Take a piece of paper or open a note on your phone and write two short lists:

List 1: "Cheese That Was Moved Without My Consent"
- Jobs, roles, relationships, health changes, community shifts, closed doors.

List 2: "Cheese I Am Still Gripping, Even Though It's Gone"
- Identities, expectations, routines, versions of yourself you are still trying to resurrect.

List 3: "Cheese I Chose to Move"

These are changes you initiated or agreed to, even if you now have mixed feelings about them:
- Jobs you resigned from
- Relationships you ended or stepped back from
- Boundaries you set that changed access to you
- Cities, churches, communities, or roles you chose to leave
- Habits, expectations, or versions of yourself you decided to outgrow

For each one, you might gently ask yourself: "Why did I move this cheese at the time? What was I trying to protect or honor?" "What part of that choice I still stand by?" "What, if anything, would I do differently knowing what I know now?" This list matters because:

It honors your agency —you are not only a person things happen to; you are also a person who makes moves.

It surfaces mixed emotions —you can feel both relief and grief about cheese you chose to move.

It keeps you out of all-or-nothing thinking —you are neither only a victim nor only to blame; you are a complex human navigating a complex life. You don't have to show these lists to anyone. This is not homework for performance. It is a mirror for clarity. After you write them, sit quietly for a moment and simply acknowledge, "This changed. I didn't choose it. It matters to me." Take a few slow breaths. Put a hand on your chest if that feels okay and notice that, even with all that moved cheese, your heart is still beating. You are still here.

You may not feel anything dramatic. That's okay. All you did was open a window in a stuffy room. Fresh air rarely shouts. It just starts to move. Now, if you have a little more room, there is one more list worth noticing. List 3: "Cheese I Chose to Move" Not every change in your life happened to you. Some of it came from you. There are jobs you resigned from. Relationships you ended or quietly backed away from. Cities, churches, and communities you decided to leave. Roles you outgrew. Boundaries you finally set that changed how people could access you. Sometimes you moved that cheese out of exhaustion. Sometimes out of wisdom. Sometimes out of fear. Sometimes out of a mix so tangled you couldn't name it then and still struggle to name it now. This third list is not here to put you on trial. It is here to recognize your agency. You are not only the person standing in an empty kitchen asking, "Who moved my cheese?" You are also the person who has, at times, picked up the cheese with your own hands and said, "Not here. Not like this. Not anymore." As you think about the cheese you chose to move, you might ask yourself:

- "What was I trying to protect when I made that choice?"
- "What part of me was I trying to honor?"
- "What, if anything, do I still stand by?"

- "What, if anything, would I do differently with the insight I have now?"

You are allowed to feel more than one thing about your own decisions:

- Relief that you left.

- Grief that it had to end.

- Pride that you finally spoke up.

- Regret about how you spoke up.

Mixed feelings do not mean you made the wrong choice. They mean you are a whole human being who can see more of the picture now than you could back then. So as you sit with all three lists—Cheese that was moved without your consent, Cheese you are still gripping, even though it's gone and Cheese you chose to move. if you can offer yourself the same sentence in each category: "I did the best I could with what I knew and what I had at the time. Now that I know more, I'm allowed to grow." You don't have to rewrite your whole story tonight. You don't have to decide, in one sitting, whether every move was "right" or "wrong." For now, it is enough to tell the truth:

- Some cheese was taken.

- Some cheese slipped away.

- Some cheese, I moved myself.

All of it shaped you. None of it has to define the rest of your life. In the next chapters, we will talk about how to respond when you realize the cheese is not coming back the way it was. We will explore what it looks like to move— not in panic, not in denial, but with as much honesty, courage, and self-respect as you can carry. For now, if all you've done is admit, "My map doesn't work anymore," you have already taken a step. And in a season when everything feels like it's been taken from you, claiming even one small, truthful step is an act of quiet rebellion against despair.

CHEESE CHECK

You don't have to share these answers with anyone. Just be honest.

What's one change that happened to you—not one you started?

Write it in a sentence:

"When ___________ happened, my cheese was moved."

What did that change really take from you?

Not just the job, title, or relationship. Did it take identity, community, routine, security, control, trust? Circle the one that stings the most.

Where have you been pointing the finger?

At a person? A group? "The system"? God? Yourself? How has that story helped you survive so far?

How is it keeping you from asking, "What now?"

If you could say anything—uncensored—to the person/people/circumstances that moved your cheese, what would you say?

Write the unedited version. You don't have to be "nice" on the page.

Now, if you spoke to yourself with both truth and kindness, what would you say?

"Here's what I wish I had seen…" "Here's what I did the best I could with…" "Here's what I want to do differently next time…"

What would support look like for you in this season?

A therapist? A pastor? A coach? A support group? One honest friend? What is one small step you can take this week toward that support?

You are not behind. You are not disqualified. You are a human being in the middle of a story that is still being written. In the next chapter, we'll look at the question underneath all the blame and shock: Not just ***"Who moved my cheese?"*** but "Given where I am now… what am I going to do, and why?"

CHEESE CHECK NOTES

"Sometimes the moved cheese is not a punishment.

It's an eviction notice from a place you had already outgrown."

Dr. Laide R. Alexander

CHAPTER TWO

The Question Behind the Question

When your cheese first gets moved, the loudest question is: ***"Who did this?"*** *Who made this decision? Who forgot about me? Who failed me? Who lied? Who left? Who dropped the ball?* That's normal. Your brain is trying to make sense of a world that suddenly doesn't match the map in your head. But here's the problem; If you stay with only that question, your whole life becomes an investigation scene. **You're the detective. You're the witness. You're also the victim.** And while you're building your case, the clock is still ticking on your life. At some point—usually quietly, usually when you're tired of hearing yourself tell the same story—another question starts to whisper: "Okay… but what am I going to do now?" That's the question behind the question.

Blame Is a Beginning, Not a Destination. Let's be clear: asking *"Who moved my cheese?"* is not wrong. It can even be helpful. It can reveal patterns of injustice. It can expose unhealthy systems. It can protect you from repeating old mistakes with new people. But blame is supposed to be a rest stop, not your permanent address. If you live there too long, a few things happen: Your energy gets stuck in the past. You rehearse the story over and over, but nothing in your present changes. Your identity shrinks to your injury.

You become "the one who got fired," "the one whose spouse left," "the one the church hurt," "the one whose family never supported them." Your imagination shuts down. You forget you ever had dreams, preferences, or options.

Everything is about what they did. Blame says, *"Look at what happened to me."* Agency says, *"Given what happened, here's what I choose next."* The question behind the question is the door from one to the other. **The three questions life keeps asking;** when your cheese is moved, life doesn't just ask, "Who did this?" Life quietly asks three deeper questions: *What is really over? What is still possible? Who do you want to be now?* We rarely answer these directly. Instead, we: Start another job. Join another church. Get into another relationship. Move to another city, or stay exactly where we are, but shut down emotionally. We change scenery without changing the script. This book is your chance to pause and answer those questions on purpose, so your next chapter isn't just a remix of the last one. Let's walk through them.

Question 1: *What Is Really Over?*

Not everything ends just because some things ended. But when your cheese moves, it can feel like everything is gone:

- "My whole life is falling apart."

- "Nothing is working."

- "I have to start from zero."

That may be how it feels. It is rarely the whole truth. Ask yourself:

- What exactly ended? A job? A title? A season? A version of me?

- What commitments, expectations, and routines came with that ending?

- What did I think this role/relationship/place would guarantee me… that it actually never could?

Sometimes, what's really over is:

- Your time in a particular position, not your entire career.

- Your role in a specific church, not your faith.

- A marriage as it was, not your capacity to love or be loved.

- Your ability to pretend, not your right to exist.

Naming what is actually over helps you stop trying to resurrect things that are done—and frees your energy for what is not.

Here's a sentence to try:

"This chapter is over: ______________________. My life is not over. I am still here."

It sounds simple. It is not. But it's the first crack in the wall of "*My life is ruined.*"

Question 2: *What Is Still Possible?*

When your cheese gets moved, your brain tends to highlight loss and limit:

- "I'll never find another job like that."

- "No one will ever love me like that again."

- "I'm too old to start over."

- "If I leave, I'll never find a community like this."

Some of that grief is real. Some of it is your fear talking with a megaphone. Either way, you won't see possibility until you ask for it. A simple starting point:

- What can I still do?

- What do I still know?

- Who still loves me?

- What strengths, experiences, and lessons did I gain from the thing that ended?

- What have I always wanted to try—but didn't, because I was busy protecting the old cheese?

This is not about being fake-positive. You can say, in the same breath; "I lost something I really wanted. And I still have a life that can hold something good." **Both are true**. You might discover that some doors you begged God to keep open were actually keeping you from walking through others.

Sometimes the moved cheese is not a punishment. It's an eviction notice from a place you had already outgrown.

Question 3: *Who Do You Want to Be Now?*

This is the heart of the question behind the question.

Not: "What do I want people to think about me?", "How do I prove them wrong?", "How do I show them I'm still valuable?" However, "Given what happened, and given who I know I am becoming, who do I want to be now?" Because truthfully, you have options. After the divorce, you can become: *Bitter and closed* or *wiser and clearer* about your needs. After the job loss, you can become: *Cynical and checked-out* or *more honest about what you're called to do.* After the church hurt, you can become: *Anti-everything* or *more discerning and anchored in what you truly believe.* You don't control every event, but you do participate in the person you become next. Your character is not only revealed by change; it is also formed by how you respond to it. So ask yourself:

- What kind of person do I respect when I see them go through what I'm going through?

- What stories do I want to tell about this season ten years from now?

- What do I want my children, friends, or community to learn from how I handled this?

These questions shift you from; *"Why did this happen to me?"* to *"Who am I choosing to be in the middle of it?"* That's a very different conversation.

Two Roads After *"Who Moved My Cheese?"* Let's make this practical. After your cheese is moved, you stand at a fork in the road:

ROAD 1 — The Loop

You keep asking, *"Who moved my cheese?"*
You collect proof.
You replay the story.
You gather people who agree with you.

Years pass. You are still telling the same story, just with better vocabulary.

ROAD 2 —The Question Behind the Question

You honor what happened.

You name what you lost.

You tell the truth about who did what.

And then you ask:

- What is really over?

- What is still possible?

- Who do I want to be now?

On Road 1, other people's choices define you. *On Road 2*, other people's choices impact you—but they don't get the last word. You may still need time on Road 1. That's okay. There is no rush. But at some point, staying there will start to feel like wearing clothes that are too tight. When that happens, that's your soul saying, "It's time to ask a better question."

Honesty Break: What If I Don't Want to Ask Better Questions? Let's be very honest. Sometimes, we don't want to be the bigger person. We don't want to grow. We want justice, or revenge, or a refund.

We want:

- The job back

- The relationship fixed

- The apology we never got

- The time we lost

And underneath that, we want something even more basic: **We want the world to make sense again.** Asking deeper questions can feel like letting people off the hook. *It's not.* You can: Hold people accountable, set boundaries, seek justice where possible, tell the truth about what happened, and still refuse to let what they did be the only thing shaping who you become. Growth is not letting them off the hook. Growth is taking yourself off their hook. You are more than what they did.

A New Question for Your Next Move. Spencer Johnson, M.D., gave the world a powerful, simple question: ***"Who moved my cheese?"*** Your life is inviting you to add another; *"Given that my cheese has been moved, what am I going to do now, and why?"* That second question is where your power lives. It doesn't erase what you've been through. It doesn't guarantee a smooth road ahead. But it does shift your posture from: *"I'm just trying to survive what they did"* to *"I am actively choosing how I move from here."* In the next part of this book, we'll look at the different ways people move their cheese: To survive. To grow. To hide. And by quietly letting others move it for them. But before we go there, take a moment with your own life and listen for the question behind the question.

Sitting in the Ruins of Your Old Map. When your cheese moves, it's not just the loss of a thing. It's the loss of a map. You had an inner picture of how life was "supposed" to go:

- "If I work hard and stay loyal, I'll be secure."
- "If I love well and do my part, this relationship will last."
- "If I serve faithfully, the church will cover me."
- "If I save, plan, and pray, my future will be stable."

When reality stops matching that picture, you don't just grieve the loss—you grieve the story you were telling yourself. That's why the pain feels so disorienting. You're not only asking, "Who moved my cheese?" You're asking, "Can I trust my own judgment? Can I trust God? Can I trust people? Can I trust myself?" This is where the question behind the question becomes more than a mindset shift. It becomes spiritual and emotional surgery. Because now you're not just deciding what to do next. You're deciding what you will believe next.

The Hidden Cost of Staying in "Who Moved My Cheese?" Let's be honest about the price of staying at the surface question. When you live in "Who moved my cheese?" too long, it doesn't just shape your thoughts. It reshapes your nervous system.

You become:

- **Hyper-vigilant** —always scanning for who might hurt you next.

- **Suspicious** —assuming motives before you have facts.

- **Defensive** —reacting to small things as if they are big threats.

- **Numb** —checking out so you don't have to feel disappointed again.

You may call it "wisdom" or "having my guard up," but sometimes it's just unprocessed pain wearing grown-up clothes. You are not weak for starting with blame. You are human. But you will feel weaker if you never move beyond it. The question behind the question is not about pretending nothing happened. It's about refusing to give your wound permanent authority over your future.

When the Story Becomes the Cage. Every hurt comes with a story. "They didn't value me." "I was never enough." "They always choose them over me." "Every time I trust, I get burned." Some of those stories are accurate descriptions of what happened. But over time, they can turn into predictions:

- "They didn't value me" quietly becomes "No one will ever truly value me."

- "I was never enough for them" becomes "I will never be enough for anyone."

- "This church hurt me" becomes "All churches are dangerous."

- "This leader betrayed me" becomes "All leaders are corrupt."

Your brain is trying to protect you. It would rather overgeneralize than risk another surprise. The problem is, those protective stories become bars on a cage you didn't mean to build. The question behind the question walks you to the lock and gently asks, "Is this still true? Is this the only possible story? Who do I want to be now, even if this story has some truth in it?" You don't have to deny the pain to question the prison it built.

Grief, Anger, and the Question Behind the Question. Let's talk about grief and anger, because they are often the loudest voices after your cheese moves. Grief says: "Something precious is gone." "That season will never come back." "I miss what we had, even if it wasn't perfect." *Anger says:* "This was unfair." "I deserved better." "They should have handled this differently."

Both grief and anger are valid. They are not your enemies. In fact, they are often advocates for your heart. They stand up and say, "What happened mattered. You mattered." But here's what they are not designed to do: Grief is not designed to be your permanent identity. Anger is not designed to be your permanent operating system. If you fuse your identity with your grief, you become "the one who lost." If you fuse your identity with your anger, you become "the one who fights." The question behind the question invites grief and anger to sit at the table—but not to sit on the throne. You can say:

- "I am grieving. And I am still becoming."

- "I am angry. And I am still responsible for my next move."

That shift alone is revolutionary.

The Quiet Power of Naming Reality. One of the most powerful things you can do after your cheese moves is simply to tell the truth, without drama and without editing. Try statements like:

- "I was laid off."

- "My marriage ended."

- "That church wounded me."

- "That friendship is over."

- "I was overlooked for that opportunity."

Notice what's missing: adjectives and predictions. No:

- "I was unfairly laid off, and my career is ruined."

- "My marriage ended, so I'll probably be alone forever."

- "That church wounded me; all churches are toxic."

There may be some truth in those adjectives and predictions, but when you fuse them to the event, you stop being able to see anything else. The question behind the question starts with clean truth:

- "This is what happened."
- "This is how it impacted me."
- "This is what I feel about it."

And then asks:

- "Given all of that… what is really over?"
- "What is still possible?"
- "Who do I want to be now?"

Clean truth is the ground. The question behind the question is the path.

Why "What Am I Going to Do Now?" Feels So Scary. You might wonder, "If this question is so powerful, why do I resist it?" Because "What am I going to do now?" exposes a few things we'd rather not look at: That no one is coming to fix it for us. That some of what we lost is truly gone. That we have more power than we are comfortable admitting. That we might have to release the role of the innocent, helpless victim. Sometimes it feels easier to stay in the courtroom of "Who moved my cheese?" because in that room, our job is clear: build the case, prove the point, wait for the verdict. But in the room of "What am I going to do now?" there is no judge, no jury, no guaranteed apology. There is only you, God, your values, your history, and your future. That level of freedom can feel like standing on a high ledge with no railing. This is why many people will choose familiar misery over unfamiliar possibilities. At least they know the script. The question behind the question invites you to write a new script—even if your hand is shaking while you hold the pen.

Micro-Moves: When You Don't Feel Ready for Big Decisions. You might be thinking, "I hear you, but I'm not ready to make big moves. I'm barely getting out of bed." Good. Let's not start with big moves. The question behind the question does not always demand massive action. Sometimes it simply asks for a micro-move—the smallest next step that honors who you want to be. A micro-move could look like:

- Sending one email to ask for information about a class, a job, or a resource.
- Making one counseling appointment.
- Going for a 10-minute walk instead of scrolling for another hour.
- Writing down, "This is what ended. This is what did not end."
- Telling one safe person the truth about what you're going through.

Micro-moves don't look impressive on social media, but they re-train your nervous system to believe, "I am not stuck. I can still move, even in small ways." The question behind the question is not, "How will I rebuild my entire life by Friday?" It is, "What is one small step I can take today that aligns with who I want to become?"

When Other People Don't Change. Sometimes we delay asking better questions because we are waiting on someone else:

- "When they apologize, then I'll move on."
- "When they finally see my value, then I'll start over."
- "When the company changes leadership, then I'll try again."
- "When my family supports me, then I'll take the next step."
- You may get all of that. Or you may not.

But here's the hard truth: your next chapter cannot be held hostage by someone else's growth curve. **You can absolutely: Pray for change. Advocate for justice. Set clear boundaries. Hope for reconciliation.** But the question behind the question is about your stewardship, not their transformation. "Given that they may or may not ever change, who do I want to be now? What is still possible for my life, regardless of what they choose?" This is not abandoning hope for others. It is refusing to abandon responsibility for yourself.

Faith, God, and Moved Cheese. If you're a person of faith, there's another layer to all of this. When the cheese moves, you might quietly ask: "God, where were You?", "Why did You let this happen?", "Why didn't You stop it?", "Why didn't You answer the way I expected?" These are not "bad Christian" questions. They are human questions. They are Bible questions. People have been asking them for thousands of years. Sometimes, in spiritual environments, we are taught to skip over the raw questions and jump straight to the "right" answers: "God is in control." "Everything happens for a reason." "It will all work out." Those may be true in a big-picture sense, but when they are used too quickly, they can feel like spiritual duct tape over a deep wound. The question behind the question with God might sound like: *"Given what I've been through, who do I believe God is now?", "What have I learned about God's presence in suffering?", "What do I want my relationship with God to look like in this new season?"* You are allowed to bring your confusion, anger, and disappointment to God. Honest questions are not an enemy of faith; they are often the doorway to a deeper, more mature faith.

From Why Me? to What Now? Let's put it all together. "Who moved my cheese?" is really a version of *"Why me?"*

- Why my job?
- Why my family?
- Why my health?
- Why my marriage?
- Why my ministry?

Sometimes you will get clear answers. Often, you will not. But "What am I going to do now, and why?" is a question you can always answer, even in the dark. It sounds like:

- "I don't know why they chose them over me. What I'm going to do now is honor my gifts, sharpen my skills, and pursue spaces that see my value."

- "I don't know why this relationship ended the way it did. What I'm going to do now is heal, learn, and refuse to carry this wound into the next person's life."

- "I don't know why this door closed. What I'm going to do now is stay open to the next door, even if it looks different than I imagined."

- "Why me?" keeps you circling the event. "What now?" starts to move your feet.

A Practice: Writing Your Next-Move Statement. Before you move into the next chapter of this book, take a moment to practice the question behind the question with a real situation in your life. Think of one area where your cheese has moved—a job, relationship, opportunity, community, identity, or dream. Then, write three short statements:

What is really over?

"This chapter is over: ___________________________."

What is still possible?

"Even now, it is still possible that _______________."

Who do I want to be now?

"In light of what happened, I choose to become someone who ___________________."

You don't have to show this to anyone. You don't have to get it "right." It will evolve as you do. The power is not in the perfection of the words, but in the fact that you are choosing to answer on purpose. You are no longer just the detective, the witness, or the victim in the story. You are also the author. And authors ask different questions. As you move into the next part of this book, keep listening for that quiet, insistent invitation underneath every loss, every surprise, every shift:

"Given that the cheese has moved… what am I going to do now, and why?"

That is the question behind the question. And it's the one that will carry you into your next move.

CHEESE CHECK

Find a quiet spot if you can. Be as unfiltered as possible.

Right now, where are you living—on **Road 1 (the loop)** or **Road 2 (the deeper questions)**?

What are the clues? How often do you tell the story of *"who moved your cheese"* vs. *imagining what's next?*

What, specifically, feels "over" in this season? Finish the sentence three times:

"This is over: ___________."

"This is over: ___________."

"This is over: ___________."

Then add: **"My life is not over. I am still here."**

List three things that are still possible for you, even after what happened. They don't have to be huge. Think in terms of:

- "I can still learn…"
- "I can still love…"
- "I can still create…"
- "I can still become…"

Who do you want to be in this chapter of your story? Choose 3 words that describe the version of you you're aiming toward (for example: honest, courageous, grounded, joyful, wise, kind, bold).

Write: "In this season, I choose to become more ________, ________, and ________."

What is one small action that matches who you say you want to be? If you chose **"honest,"** what conversation do you need to stop avoiding? If you chose **"courageous,"** what is one risk you can take this month? If you chose **"grounded,"** what practice (prayer, exercise, therapy, journaling) can you commit to?

What question have you been avoiding because you're afraid of the answer? Write it down. That question is probably the door to your next level of freedom. You don't have to fix everything today.

But you can start asking better questions today. In the next chapter, we'll look at the first way many of us move our cheese:

We move it to survive.

And sometimes, survival itself is a holy thing.

CHEESE CHECK NOTES

"Survival is not rebellion.

Sometimes, survival is obedience to the truth"

Dr. Laide R. Alexander

CHAPTER THREE

I Moved My Cheese to Survive

Not every move is a "new vision" move. Some moves are not about chasing a dream. They're about staying alive—physically, emotionally, spiritually, or mentally. No vision board. No grand announcement. Just a quiet, desperate sentence; "If I stay here, I will not be okay." So, you move. You leave the job. You step away from the ministry. You walk out of the relationship. You change your number. You say, "I can't do this anymore." From the outside, people might say: "You're overreacting." "You should have stayed and worked it out." "You just don't like commitment. "You're being dramatic." They don't know what you know; What your body felt like every morning. How much of yourself you had to swallow to keep the peace. How close you were to breaking for real. Sometimes, moving your cheese is not selfish. It's self-preservation.

When "Staying" Is Actually Disappearing. We are often praised for staying: "You're so loyal." "You're such a ride-or-die." "You're so strong." "You're so faithful." But there is a version of "staying" that is just slowly disappearing. You stay in; *A job that pays you but starves your soul. A relationship that calls you everything but your name. A ministry that loves your gift but ignores your humanity. A family role where you are the responsible one, the fixer, the strong one—until you are empty.* On paper, you are still there. In reality, pieces of you have been leaving for years. You stop laughing the way you used to. You stop dreaming. You stop telling the truth. You stop recognizing yourself. Eventually, one of two things will move; The situation will change you beyond recognition, or you will change the situation by moving your cheese. Survival moves often look sudden to other people. They are rarely sudden to you.

The Secret Calculations No One Sees. Before a survival move, there are usually months or years of silent math. You lie awake at night doing equations in your head; *"If I stay, what is this costing me?" "If I leave, what will it cost them?" "If I say something, will it get better or worse?" "If I don't say anything, how long can I keep pretending?"* You count; The bills, the children, the reputation, the years you've invested, the "what will people say?", the "what will church people say?", the "what will my family say?", you rehearse tiny trial moves: "What if I just cut back my hours?" "What if we separate for a while?" "What if I take a break from serving?" "What if I move to the guest room… then the couch… then out?" From the outside, all people see is the day you act. From the inside, you know this was the day you finally stopped ignoring your own alarm system.

Your Body Knows Before Your Brain Admits It. Survival moves rarely start in your head. They start in your body. Your body has been filing complaints for a long time:

- Headaches that never quite go away

- Sunday-night dread for a Monday-morning job

- Tears in the parking lot before you walk into the building

- A tight chest every time a certain person calls your name

- Numbness where joy used to live

Your body has been whispering:

- "We can't keep doing this."

- "I'm tired."

- "This is not safe."

- "This is not home."

But your mind has been trained to shout back:

- "People are depending on you."

- "You're being too sensitive."

- "Other people have it worse."

- "God wouldn't bring you here just to leave you."

- "You made a commitment. You can't just walk away."

So you override the alarms. Again. And again. And again. When you finally move your cheese to survive, you are not impulsive. *You are finally listening.*

Survival Is Not a Sin. Let's address something directly, especially for those raised on a heavy diet of "self-sacrifice": Choosing not to die in a situation is not selfish. It is not disloyal. It is not a lack of faith.

Sometimes, the most spiritual thing you can do is leave:

- Leave the abuse.

- Leave the manipulation.

- Leave the chronic disrespect.

- Leave the place where you are shrinking so small you can barely be seen.

We love to quote: *"I can do all things through Christ who strengthens me."* We forget: That does not mean, "I can stay anywhere, under anything, forever, with no consequences." God did not create you just to be a durable punching bag. *Yes, there are seasons where we endure. Yes, there are burdens we carry for love. Yes, there are commitments we fight for.* But there is a line between carrying a cross and climbing onto one someone else built for their convenience. Survival is not rebellion. Sometimes, survival is obedience to the truth.

The Guilt That Comes With Saving Yourself. Even when you move to survive, guilt usually comes along for the ride. You may think:

- "Maybe I should have stayed a little longer."

- "Maybe I'm the problem."

- "Good parents/spouses/workers/ministers don't leave."
- "If I were stronger, I could have handled it."

And people may help that guilt along:

- "You just walked away?"
- "But we needed you."
- "You're abandoning us."
- "After everything they did for you…"
- "You're not being Christian enough / loyal enough / grateful enough."

Here's a gentle but firm truth: The people who benefited from your silence, over-functioning, or self-erasure will often experience your survival as betrayal. That does not mean you betrayed them. It means the old version of you—the one who tolerated too much—is gone. You have a right to miss them. You do not have to go back to dying to make them comfortable.

When Survival Moves Hurt People You Love. Now, let's be honest about another layer:

- Your survival move may hurt people you care about.
- Children who have to navigate a new family structure.
- Coworkers who feel your absence.
- Congregations who miss your leadership.
- Partners who are suddenly confronted with consequences.
- Friends or family who depended on your role.

Survival moves can be both necessary and painful for others. Two things can be true at once: *"I had to move to live." "My move created real loss for other people."* Maturity holds both. You don't have to deny other people's pain to honor your own. You don't have to deny your need to live to acknowledge their disappointment. What you can do is: Be as honest as is safe about why you moved, take responsibility for the parts that truly belong to you, refuse to take responsibility for other people's refusal to see the full picture, you are allowed to say: *"I am sorry this hurts you. And I still cannot stay in what is killing me."*

Not Every Emergency Move Is Forever. Sometimes a survival move is permanent. Sometimes it's a necessary *pause.* You may:

- Move out before you decide if the relationship is over

- Take a leave of absence before you decide whether to resign

- Step away from serving before you know if you'll return

- Take a job that's not your "dream" just to stabilize for a season

That's okay. Every move doesn't have to be a final declaration. Sometimes it's a lifeboat, not the cruise ship. You are allowed to say: "This is what I can do for now.", "This is the boundary I need for this season.", "I don't know the long-term plan yet. I just know I can't keep doing that." Survival buys you time to see clearly. Clarity rarely comes while you're drowning.

When Survival Turns Into Hiding. There is one warning we need to name. A survival move is healthy, when it: Protects your life, health, or sanity, moves you out of active harm, creates space for healing, reflection, and growth. A survival move turns into hiding when: *You never do the healing or reflection. You start running from anything that reminds you of the past. You use "protecting my peace" as a way to avoid every hard conversation or new risk.* Sometimes we say "I'm just surviving" when what we mean is: *"I don't ever want to feel that kind of pain again, so I will live a smaller life to avoid it."* This book will come back to that in the chapter *"I Moved My Cheese to Hide."* For now, just remember:

- Moving to survive is a beginning, not an end.

- Survival is the first floor.

- You were not meant to live your whole life in the emergency room.

You Are Allowed to Outgrow What Once Saved You. Here is a truth that can be hard to swallow: The move that saved you in one season may limit you in the next. The walls you built to protect yourself can become a prison.

The "I don't need anybody" mindset that kept you from going back can keep you from letting new, healthy people in. The hyper-independence that helped you survive can make you unwilling to receive help. You are allowed to say: *"That decision saved my life then. And now I'm ready to live, not just survive."* Honoring your survival move doesn't mean you're stuck with every defense mechanism that came with it. You get to keep the wisdom and release the fear. Not every move is a "new vision" move. Some moves are not about chasing a dream. They're about staying alive—physically, emotionally, mentally. No vision board. No grand announcement. Just a quiet, desperate sentence: "If I stay here, I will not be okay." So, you move. You leave the job. You step away from the role. You walk out of the relationship. You change your number. You say, "I can't do this anymore." From the outside, people might say:

- "You're overreacting."
- "You should have stayed and worked it out."
- "You just don't like commitment."
- "You're being dramatic."

They don't know what you know:

- What your body felt like every morning.
- How much of yourself you had to swallow to keep the peace.
- How many times you rehearsed resigning in the shower.
- How close you were to breaking for real.

Sometimes, moving your cheese is not selfish. It's self-preservation.

When "Staying" Is Actually Disappearing. In corporate culture, "staying" gets you awards. "Loyalty bonus." "Ten-year service plaque." "We couldn't have done it without you." "You're such a team player." But there is a version of "staying" that is just slowly disappearing. You stay in:

- A job that pays you but starves your mind.
- A role that calls you "high potential" but never promotes you.

- A team that loves your output but ignores your burnout.
- A family role where you are the reliable one, the fixer, the strong one—until you are empty.

On paper, you are still there. In reality, pieces of you have been leaving for years. You stop raising your hand in meetings. You stop pitching ideas because you already know how the story ends. You stop laughing the way you used to. You stop dreaming about what's next. You stop telling the truth about how you're actually doing. Eventually, one of two things will move:

The situation will change you beyond recognition, or *You will change the situation by moving your cheese.* Survival moves often look sudden to other people. They are rarely sudden to you.

The Secret Calculations No One Sees. Before a survival move, there are usually months or years of silent math. You lie awake at night doing equations in your head: "If I stay, what is this costing me?" "If I leave, what will it cost them?" "If I speak up, will it get better or worse?" "If I don't say anything, how long can I keep pretending?" "If I quit, how many months of savings do I actually have?" *You count:*

- The mortgage or rent.
- The kids' tuition.
- The health insurance.
- The reputation you've built.
- The LinkedIn optics.
- The "What will my family say?"
- The "What will my mentors think?"
- The "How will this look on my résumé?"

You rehearse tiny trial moves: "What if I just cut back my hours?" "What if I move to a different department?" "What if I ask for a sabbatical?" "What if we separate for a while?" "What if I move to the guest room... then the couch… then out?" From the outside, all people see is the day you act. From the inside, you know that was the day you finally stopped ignoring your own alarm system.

Your Body Knows Before Your Brain Admits It. Survival moves rarely start in your head. They start in your body. Your body has been filing complaints for a long time: Headaches that never quite go away. Sunday-night dread for a Monday-morning job. Tears in the parking garage before you badge in. A tight chest every time a certain name appears in your inbox. That sinking feeling when the calendar invite says "quick sync" with no agenda. Numbness where joy used to live.

Your body has been whispering: "We can't keep doing this." "I'm tired." "This isn't safe." "This is not home." But your mind has been trained to shout back:

- "People are depending on you."
- "You're being too sensitive."
- "Other people have it worse."
- "This is just how corporate life is."
- "You made a commitment. You can't just walk away."
- "This is the industry. Toughen up."

So you override the alarms. Again. And again. And again. You drink more coffee. You scroll more at night. You call it "just a busy season" for the seventh quarter in a row. When you finally move your cheese to survive, you are not being impulsive. You are finally listening.

Survival Is Not a Performance Issue. Let's address something directly, especially for high-achievers and over-performers: Choosing not to burn out is not laziness. Leaving a toxic culture is not "quitting on your dream." Refusing to be chronically disrespected is not having a bad attitude. Saying "no more" is not a lack of grit. In many workplaces, overextension is branded as "passion." Exhaustion is rebranded as "hustle." Boundaryless availability is labeled "leadership potential." You get praised for answering emails at midnight. You get promoted for doing two jobs for the price of one. You get thanked for "stepping up" in every crisis—which never seems to end. We confuse endurance with health. We confuse sacrifice with strategy. We confuse being needed with being valued. Sometimes, the most professional, grown-up, responsible thing you can do is leave:

- Leave the leader who only knows how to manage by fear.

- Leave the team that keeps calling trauma "a fast-paced environment."

- Leave the role that has no ceiling because it was never supposed to be a role—it was a gap they realized you were willing to fill.

Survival is not a performance issue. Sometimes, survival is the only metric that proves you're fully awake.

The Guilt That Comes With Saving Yourself. Even when you move to survive, guilt usually packs itself in your carry-on. You may think: "Maybe I should have stayed a little longer." "Maybe I'm the common denominator." "Good leaders/employees/partners don't leave." "If I were stronger, I could have handled it.", "Other people seem to be fine. What's wrong with me?" And people may help that guilt along: "You just walked away?" "But we were counting on you." "After everything this company did for you…""You know how this looks, right?" "You're burning bridges." Here's a hard but freeing truth: *The people who benefited from your over-functioning, silence, or self-erasure will often experience your survival as betrayal.* That doesn't mean you betrayed them. It means the old version of you—the one who tolerated too much—is gone. You have a right to miss that version. You do not have to resurrect it. You are allowed to say: "I am sorry this hurts you. And I still cannot stay in what is killing me."

When Survival Moves Hurt People You Love. Now for the uncomfortable part: sometimes your survival move creates real pain for people who did not create the problem. Children who have to adjust to a new family rhythm. A partner who has to face their own behavior without your buffering. Coworkers who feel abandoned in a difficult season. A manager who relied on you to hold a shaky team together. Aging parents who don't understand why you won't "just stay a little longer." Two things can be true at once: "I had to move to live." "My move created loss for other people." *Maturity holds both.*

You don't have to deny other people's pain to honor your own. You don't have to deny your need to live in order to acknowledge their disappointment. What you can do is: Be as honest as is safe about why you moved. Take responsibility for what is truly yours (poor communication, delayed decisions, mixed signals). Refuse to take responsibility for what is not yours (their denial, their unwillingness to see red flags, their choice to ignore your earlier warnings). *You are allowed to say:*

- "I care about how this impacts you.
- And I care about not vanishing from my own life."

Not Every Emergency Move Is Forever. Sometimes a survival move is permanent. Sometimes it's a necessary pause. You may:

- Move out before you decide if the relationship is over.
- Take a leave of absence before you decide whether to resign.
- Step away from serving before you know if you'll return.
- Take a "bridge job" that's not your dream, just to stabilize for a season.
- Downsize your life so you can upsize your sanity.

That's okay. Every move doesn't have to be a final declaration. Sometimes it's a lifeboat, not the cruise ship. You are allowed to say: "This is what I can do for now." "This is the boundary I need for this season." "I don't know the five-year plan yet. I just know I can't keep doing that." Clarity rarely shows up while you're drowning. Survival buys you time to see clearly.

When Survival Turns Into Hiding. There is one warning we need to name. A survival move is healthy when it: Protects your life, health, or mental stability. Moves you out of active harm. Creates space for healing, reflection, and growth. A survival move turns into hiding when:

- You never do the healing or reflection.
- You refuse every opportunity that looks even remotely like the past.
- You use "protecting my peace" as a universal excuse to avoid hard conversations, feedback, or growth.
- "Never again" quietly becomes "I will never risk again."

Sometimes we say "I'm just surviving" when what we mean is:

"I don't ever want to feel that kind of pain again, so I will live a smaller life to avoid it."

You stop applying for roles you're qualified for. You stop letting anyone close enough to disappoint you. You stop asking more of your life than "not terrible." This book will come back to that in the chapter *"I Moved My Cheese to Hide."* For now, just remember:

- Moving to survive is a beginning, not an endpoint.
- Survival is the first floor.
- You were not meant to live your whole life in the emergency room.

Self-Awareness: What Did This Place Turn You Into? Survival moves are not just about where you go. They're about who you were becoming before you left.

Ask yourself:

- "Who was I turning into in that environment?"
- "What did I have to mute in myself to make this work?"
- "What did I start believing about my worth, intelligence, or potential?"
- "If I had stayed five more years, who would I have become?"

Be specific:

- "I became someone who apologized for asking fair questions."
- "I became someone who checked my email before I brushed my teeth."

- "I became someone who believed rest was a reward, not a right."
- "I became someone who thought being constantly anxious was normal."
- "I became someone who only felt valuable when I was fixing a crisis."

That self-awareness is not for self-blame. It's for data. Because if you don't know who you were becoming there, you won't know what to watch for in the next place.

Accountability: What Was Your Part?

Survival doesn't cancel accountability. Yes, there may have been real dysfunction, toxicity, or abuse. And: Where did you say "yes" when you meant "no"? Where did you stay silent when you knew you should speak? Where did you ignore the first (or tenth) red flag because the benefits were good? Where did you trade your own boundaries for belonging, status, or security? This is not about excusing bad behavior from others. It's about reclaiming your role as an active participant in your own story. Because if the only lesson from your survival move is "They were terrible," you've learned almost nothing that will protect you next time. A more honest conclusion might be: *"They behaved poorly. And I repeatedly trained them that I would tolerate it."* That's not an indictment. That's an insight. And insight is what keeps you from repeating the same script with a different cast.

The Corporate Spin Cycle: When "Culture" Is the Problem. Let's talk about the system itself. Sometimes, your survival move isn't about one villain. It's about a culture. A culture that says: "We're a family here" (translation: we expect unpaid emotional labor). We move fast and break things" (translation: people, mostly). "We hire only A-players" (translation: everyone is exhausted and replaceable). "We're scrappy" (translation: we don't plan, we just panic together).

You might have left because of one bad boss. But zoom out and you realize:

- HR was under-resourced and over-loyal to leadership.

- Boundaries were praised in theory and punished in practice.

- Burnout was treated as a personal weakness, not a structural outcome.

- Diversity was a slide in the all-hands deck, not a lived reality in the room.

When you move your cheese to survive in a corporate context, part of your growth is learning to see the water you were swimming in. Because if you don't name the water, you'll blame yourself for not being able to breathe.

Humor Break: Signs Your Cheese Needed to Move Yesterday. Sometimes the truth is easier to swallow with a little humor. If any of these feel too familiar, your cheese may be overdue for relocation:

- You've drafted your resignation letter more than three times—and saved it as "Q1_Report_Final_FINAL_v7.docx."

- Your therapist knows your org chart.

- Your smartwatch keeps asking if you're "in a workout" during staff meetings.

- You've started narrating your own life like a documentary: "Here we see the worker in its natural habitat, replying 'Sure, happy to!' while dying inside."

- You've mentally redesigned your manager's entire department structure—during meetings they're running.

- Your out-of-office reply is more honest than your performance review.

Humor doesn't fix it. But it does tell you something important:
Part of you is still alive enough to notice how absurd this is. That's good news.

Strategic Survival vs. Emotional Fleeing. Not every exit is the same. Some people leave in a blaze of emotion: no plan, no savings, a two-sentence email sent at 2:00 a.m. Others over-plan and under-leave: five-year spreadsheets, thirty versions of their résumé, and still no actual resignation. Healthy survival is a middle path: strategic and honest. Ask yourself:

- "What's my realistic runway?" (money, support, time)
- "What do I need in place to leave safely, not perfectly?"
- "Who can I talk to who has made a similar move?"
- "What's my absolute latest 'no later than' date, even if everything isn't lined up?"

Survival moves are not about winning the "Best Exit Story" competition. They're about leaving in a way that your future self will thank you for—even if present you is scared.

You Are Allowed to Outgrow What Once Saved You. Here's a truth that can be hard to swallow: The move that saved you in one season may limit you in the next. The walls you built to protect yourself can become a prison. The independence that kept you from going back can keep you from ever letting anyone in.

You are allowed to say: "That decision saved my life then. And now I'm ready to live, not just survive." Honoring your survival move doesn't mean you're stuck with every defense mechanism that came with it. You get to keep the wisdom and release the fear. You can:

- Keep the boundary, loosen the bitterness.
- Keep the lesson, drop the self-contempt.
- Keep the discernment, let go of the assumption that everyone is out to use you.

Survival was the emergency strategy. It doesn't have to be your permanent identity.

From "I Had No Choice" to "I Chose". At first, survival moves often feel like, "I had no choice." In many ways, that's true. The alternative felt like extinction. But as you gain distance, there is power in reframing: "I chose not to keep betraying myself." "I chose not to normalize disrespect." "I chose to believe that my life is bigger than this one role, company, or relationship." "I had no choice" keeps you as a character swept along by the plot. *"I chose" restores you* *as an author.* You may not have chosen all the circumstances that pushed you to the edge. But you did choose not to jump off it. You chose to move your cheese.

A Self-Audit: Was This a Survival Move? If you're not sure whether a past or current decision was a survival move, here are some questions to sit with:

What was I protecting? My health? My sanity? My safety? My sense of self?

What were the warning signs I ignored for too long? Physical symptoms? Constant dread? Loss of joy? Feedback from people who love me?

What finally made it impossible to stay? A specific event? A comment? A medical scare? A moment of seeing myself clearly?

What did I gain by leaving that I couldn't have gained by staying? Sleep? Perspective? Self-respect? Energy?

What did I lose by leaving that I'm still grieving? Status? Community? Income? Identity?

Your answers are your data. They're not a verdict on your worth. They're a map for what you need next.

From Survival to Strategy. Moving your cheese to survive is the first pivot. But if you stop there, your life becomes a series of emergency exits. The next phase is asking: "Now that I'm not in crisis, what do I want to build?" "What kind of work actually energizes me?" "What kind of relationships feel mutual, not transactional?" "What kind of leader do I never want to become, based on what I've seen?"

Survival is reactive.

Strategy is proactive.

Survival says, "Never again that."

Strategy says, "Next time, this instead." The same intelligence you used to calculate risk in the dark can be used to design a healthier life in the light.

A New Definition of Strength. For many of us, "strength" used to mean: Staying no matter what. Carrying more than is reasonable. Being the last one standing. Never asking for help. Never being the one who "gave up." After you've moved your cheese to survive, you get to redefine strength:

- Strength is telling the truth about your limits before they become emergencies.

- Strength is choosing environments where you don't have to abandon yourself to succeed.

- Strength is being willing to disappoint others in order not to disappear.

- Strength is asking for help before you collapse.

- Strength is walking away from tables where the cost of a seat is your self-respect.

That version of strength is quieter. It doesn't always get applause. But it will let you keep your life.

A Question for Your Next Move. If this chapter is stirring something in you, don't rush past it. Take one situation in your life—past or present—where you suspect you moved (or want to move) your cheese to survive.

Write down three honest sentences:

"If I had stayed, I would have lost ______________."

"By leaving, I protected ______________."

"Going forward, I will no longer trade ______________ for ______________."

You don't have to show this to anyone. You don't have to post it or justify it. This is not for your manager, your ex, your colleagues, or your family. It's for you—the part of you that finally said: *"If I stay here, I will not be okay."*

That voice is not dramatic. That voice is not weak. That voice is your life trying to save itself. Moving your cheese to survive was not the end of your story. It was your proof that, even under pressure, some part of you still knows:

I am not here just to endure. I am here to live.

CHEESE CHECK

This chapter is about telling the truth—without shame—about the moves you've made to stay alive.

Take your time. Name one move you made primarily to survive.

"I left ___________ because staying was killing ___________ in me."

Fill in those blanks honestly.

What were the alarms your body and soul were sounding before you moved? Headaches, anxiety, depression, anger, numbness, dread, loss of joy? Looking back, what were they trying to tell you? What messages made it hard for you to consider leaving?

- "Good Christians don't leave."

- "Real men/women don't quit."

- "Family is everything, no matter what."

- "If you walk away, you're ungrateful."

- Which ones still echo in your head?

Who, if anyone, experienced your survival move as betrayal? Write their names or roles. Then complete this sentence:

- "I can care about their feelings and still care about my life."

- In what ways did that survival move protect you?

- Be specific: health, sanity, safety, faith, finances, children, dignity.

Give yourself permission to say, "I saved myself."

In what ways might that survival move still be shaping how you live now?

Are there walls you built then that you don't need as high now?

Are there fears from that season that no longer match your current reality?

What would it look like to bless that past version of you instead of judging them? Write a short note to your "survival self":

"Thank you for _____________. Because of you, I am still here."

You didn't move your cheese in that season to be impressive. You moved it so you wouldn't disappear. In the next chapter, we'll talk about a different kind of move:

> **Not "I moved my cheese so I wouldn't die,"**
> **but "I moved my cheese so I could grow."**

CHEESE CHECK NOTES

Growth rarely shows up with a flashing neon sign that says,

"Time to go."

It's subtler.

Pay attention to things like restless gratitude.

Dr Laide R. Alexander

CHAPTER FOUR

I Moved My Cheese to Grow

Not every move comes from crisis. *Sometimes, nothing is "on fire."* No one is yelling. The check clears. The relationship is… fine. The church is… fine. The job is… fine. And that's the problem. You are not on the verge of collapse. You are on the verge of outgrowing your life. Something in you starts whispering:

"I'm grateful… and I'm not growing here anymore."

That whisper is easy to ignore—especially when things look stable from the outside. But over time, ignoring it can feel just as suffocating as any crisis. Growth moves are different from survival moves. They sound more like:

- "If I stay here, I won't die… but I might never really live."

- "This is good, but I know there's more."

- "I've learned what I needed to learn here. It's time for the next level."

So you start thinking about moving your cheese—not because you have to, but because you want to. And that can be even scarier.

When "Good" Becomes the Enemy of "Growing". One of the most dangerous places you can be is in a situation that is: Not abusive, not falling apart, not obviously wrong, …but no longer aligned with who you're becoming. It's… good. It's familiar. It's comfortable. You know the routines. You know the people. You know what's expected. And yet:

- You are under-challenged.
- Your gifts are underused.
- Your curiosity is underfed.
- Your spirit is underwhelmed.

You start to feel like a plant that has filled the pot. Nothing is "wrong" with the pot. You just don't have room to stretch anymore. If you stay, you won't be miserable. You'll just slowly become a smaller version of yourself. And that's its own kind of loss.

The Quiet Signs You're Outgrowing a Space. Growth rarely shows up with a flashing neon sign that says, "TIME TO GO." It's subtler. Pay attention to things like: *Restless gratitude.*

You're thankful… and restless. You can say, "I'm blessed," and still feel, "I'm not done."

Chronic boredom with what used to excite you. The work you once loved now feels like you're doing the same level over and over on a game you've already beaten. Your "what if" daydreams are getting louder. You find yourself thinking about going back to school, starting a business, changing careers, moving cities, writing the book, starting the ministry. You feel guilty for wanting more. You catch yourself thinking, "Who do I think I am, wanting that?" You're mentoring others to do what you've already mastered. You can teach it in your sleep. That's beautiful. It also means you might be ready for a new challenge. None of these automatically mean "quit tomorrow." They do mean, "Pay attention." Something in you is stretching.

The Fear of "Leaving a Good Thing". Let's be honest: growth moves can feel disrespectful to what you already have. You might think:

- "People would kill for this opportunity."
- "My parents worked hard so I could get here, and now I want to leave?"
- "What if I leave a good thing and end up with nothing?"

"Is this ambition… or ingratitude?" We are often taught to endure pain, but not how to leave comfort. Leaving something clearly bad is easier to explain:

- "They mistreated me."

- "It was toxic."

- "I had no choice."

Leaving something good is harder: "It was fine. I just knew I was done." That's not a dramatic story. But it might be a deeply honest one. Here's a truth that may stretch you: You can be grateful for a season and still outgrow it. Gratitude does not require you to stay small.

When Your Growth Threatens Other People's Comfort. Growth moves don't only affect you. They affect the people who benefit from you staying exactly where you are. When you say: "I'm going back to school." "I'm starting this business." "I'm moving." "I'm transitioning out of this role." *You might hear:*

- "Why would you do that? You have it so good here."

- "So you think you're better than us now?"

- • "You're being unrealistic."

- "At your age?"

- "You really think you can make money doing that?"

- "God gave you this; why would you walk away?"

Sometimes their concern is sincere. Sometimes their concern is really about their convenience, fear, or insecurity. Your growth can feel like a mirror to people who stopped growing a long time ago. Your job is not to shrink so they never have to look in that mirror. You can love people and still disappoint their expectations.

Discerning: Am I Growing or Just Running?. Before, you pack your bags, we need to ask an important question: "Am I moving my cheese to grow, or am I moving it to avoid something uncomfortable right here?" Because growth and avoidance can look similar on the outside:

- New job, new city, new partner, new church.
- New degree, new project, new "calling."

The difference is in your why. Growth says:

- "I've gone as far as I can at this level. I'm ready to be stretched again."
- "I'm willing to face new challenges and be a beginner again."
- "I'm willing to do the inner work, not just change scenery."

Avoidance says:

- "I don't want to have this hard conversation, so I'll just leave."
- "I don't want to look at my patterns, so I'll find a new environment that doesn't know them yet."
- "I don't want to risk failing here, so I'll go somewhere I can still pretend I might have."

Sometimes we call avoidance "growth" so it sounds better on Instagram. Only you (and maybe your therapist or trusted circle) will know the truth. A simple test: If you took this move off the table, what hard thing would you have to face right where you are? Are you willing to face that before or as you move? If the answer is no, there might be some hiding mixed into your "growth." We'll talk more about that in the "hiding" chapter. For now, just be honest with yourself.

Growth Requires Grief, Too. We usually expect grief when things are taken from us. We don't always expect grief when we freely walk away. But even growth moves come with loss: *You lose familiarity. You lose "I know exactly what I'm doing." You lose the identity you had in that space. You lose being the expert, the go-to, the one everyone knows.* You might move from: "I run this place" to "I don't even know where the bathroom is yet." You might go from: "Dr. So-and-So, Director of Such-and-Such" to "New person filling out onboarding forms." That can feel like a demotion—even if, in the long run, it's a promotion for your soul. Allow yourself to grieve: The routines you loved, the status you enjoyed, the comfort of knowing what you're doing. Grief doesn't mean you made the wrong move. It means you are human.

The Awkwardness of Being a Beginner Again. Here's a fun fact about growth: It will always make you a beginner at something. And being a beginner is humbling. You might go from: Facilitating meetings to asking where the meeting link is, preaching sermons to sitting quietly in the back row, supervising a team to asking, "Can you show me how this software works again? "Feeling fluent in your work to tripping over your words in a new field. ***If you need to always look like you know what you're doing, growth will be very hard for you.***

You will be tempted to:

- Stay where you're the expert

- Only do what you're already good at

- Call it "stewardship" when it's really fear of looking foolish

- Growth requires a little holy clumsiness.

You have to be willing to say: "I don't know yet." "Can you teach me?" "I'm new here." "This is outside my comfort zone." That doesn't mean you've lost your previous wisdom. It means you're adding to it.

Faith, Calling, and the Myth of the One Perfect Path. If you're a person of faith, growth moves can feel especially loaded. We can get tangled in questions like: *"Did God really tell me to leave?" "What if I step out of God's will?" "Is wanting more spiritual… or selfish?"* Here's something to consider: Sometimes God's guidance looks less like a detailed GPS and more like a nudge in the direction of who you're becoming. You may not get a billboard that says: ***"Thus saith the Lord: Take the job."*** You may instead get: A growing restlessness, a series of confirmations, and wise counsel that aligns with your deepest values.

Doors that open as you start moving your feet. Could you make a misstep? Of course. But you can also course-correct. You are not fragile glass that will shatter if you take one imperfect step. You are a whole human who can learn, adjust, and grow. Sometimes the only way to know if a move is right is to start moving and pay attention.

You Don't Owe Everyone a PowerPoint. One more practical note: When you move your cheese to grow, you will feel a strong pull to explain yourself to everyone. You do not owe a full TED Talk to: Every coworker, every church member, every cousin or every internet follower. You owe:

- Honesty to the people directly affected

- Clarity to yourself

- Obedience to what you know is true in your spirit

You can say: "This has been a meaningful season, and I'm grateful. It's also time for me to grow in new ways." "I don't have all the details yet, but I know I can't ignore this nudge anymore." Some people will understand only in hindsight. Some may never understand at all. You usually don't schedule a growth crisis. It shows up in the middle of a normal week. Your alarm goes off. You do the usual sequence: check email, scroll a little, consider running away to another country for three seconds, get in the shower, commute, log on. The company intranet has a banner about "Exciting New Initiatives." Your manager mentions "great momentum." Your calendar is full of recurring meetings with names like "Weekly Sync" and "Alignment Touchpoint." Everything looks exactly how it's supposed to look in a stable, functioning organization. And yet there's this small, inconvenient thought that won't leave you alone: "*I'm not supposed to be this numb.*"
You're not burnt out, exactly. You're… under-lit. That's where many growth moves really start—not with a catastrophe, but with the quiet realization that your life is working and you are not.

The Subtle Violence of "Fine". "Fine" is one of the most socially acceptable forms of self-erasure. "How's work?" "It's fine." "How's your team? They're fine." "How are you?" "I'm fine." Fine is safe. Fine doesn't alarm anyone. Fine won't get you sent to HR or to therapy. Organizations love "fine." Fine people don't rock the boat. They don't ask for much. They show up, deliver, and go home. From a distance, they look like the dream employee. From the inside, "fine" can feel like a slow leak. The danger of "fine" is not immediate ruin; it's gradual shrinkage. No one calls a meeting when you lose a little enthusiasm each quarter. There's no incident report when your standards for your own life drop by five percent a year. But give it enough time, and you wake up one morning realizing you've become an expert in a life you never consciously chose. The organization is thriving on the version of you that learned to live on half-power.

Growth as a Professional Risk, Not Just a Personal One. We like to talk about growth as if it's purely a personal journey—"finding yourself," "stepping into your purpose," all of that. But in an organizational context, growth is also a structural risk. A truly growing person will eventually ask inconvenient questions: "Why do we do it this way?" "Is this still working?" "Who benefits from this structure and who doesn't?" "What are we not talking about because it would be uncomfortable?" Those are not always career-enhancing questions. Systems are designed to preserve themselves. Even healthy ones. When you start growing, you're not just rearranging your own furniture; you're bumping into the architecture. And architecture pushes back. This is one of the reasons people unconsciously cap their own growth. Not because they're lazy, but because some part of them has already calculated the social cost of becoming larger than the role that's been assigned to them.

We don't just fear failure. We fear what will happen if we actually become as capable, clear, and honest as we suspect we could be. Because then we'd have to either ask the organization to meet us there—or leave.

Comfortable Structures and Starving Selves. Every organization has formal structures—the org chart, the reporting lines, the committees—and informal ones: who really makes decisions, whose opinion actually matters, what behavior gets rewarded, what gets quietly punished. When you first arrive, you learn those structures. You adapt. You figure out how to move inside them without getting crushed. This is normal. This is social intelligence. The problem begins when the structure that once helped you survive becomes the thing that keeps you small. Think about the first time you learned how to succeed where you are. Maybe you discovered that if you always said yes, you'd be seen as a "team player." Maybe you realized that if you stayed out of conflict, you'd be considered "easy to work with." Maybe you found that if you over-delivered, you'd be trusted with more responsibility. Those were smart moves at the time. They helped you earn trust, build capital, get traction. But fast-forward a few years, and you're still running the same strategies in a context you've outgrown. You're still saying yes by default, even when you have a better idea. You're still avoiding conflict, even when you're the most qualified person in the room to name what's not working. You're still over-delivering on tasks that don't deserve your best energy. The structure is happy. The KPIs look great. Your inner life is starving. Growth begins the moment you realize that the strategies that once kept you safe are now keeping you stuck.

When Competence Becomes a Cage. Competence is addictive. You learn your job. You get good at it. People notice. They hand you more. You handle it. They praise you. You get that little hit of "I'm needed." It feels good. Your brain loves the pattern: effort, competence, praise and, belonging. Over time, the organization builds a mental model of you: You are *the person who can always handle it." That's a compliment. And a trap.*

Because now, every time you're not sure you can handle something, you feel like you're betraying your own brand. You hesitate to volunteer for things that might expose your learning curve. You avoid roles where you'd go back to feeling awkward and slow. And suddenly, the thing that was supposed to be the natural byproduct of growth—competence—has turned into the reason you stop growing. Here's the uncomfortable truth: if you haven't felt incompetent at least once in the past year, you're probably not challenged. You don't have to chase constant anxiety. But if everything you're doing feels like a replay, if you can pull off your responsibilities with your full attention on a podcast, your life has become a museum of your former growth.

The Organization's Timeline vs. Your Timeline. Organizations move on timelines that make sense for budgets, markets, and strategic plans. You move on a timeline that makes sense for your development as a human being. And those clocks do not always sync. Your company might be in a "consolidation" phase—slowing hiring, tightening budgets, focusing on efficiency—just as you hit a "breakthrough" phase—suddenly ready for more responsibility, more stretch, more risk. Or the organization might be obsessed with speed and disruption right when you're craving depth and stability. If you assume that your growth must always align perfectly with the company's phase, you will misinterpret natural misalignments as personal failure. You'll think, "Something must be wrong with me because I'm restless while everyone else seems satisfied," or "I'm exhausted and they're calling this 'our most exciting year yet.' "It's possible that nothing is wrong with you. You may simply have reached the natural edge of what this environment can offer you at this stage. When you hit that edge, you have three options:

You can shrink your desires to fit the organization's current appetite.

You can try to drag the organization into your growth spurt (this usually ends with meetings).

Or you can accept that your timeline has shifted, and it may be time to move your cheese.

The Myth of the "Perfectly Aligned" Role. One of the most paralyzing modern ideas is the belief that somewhere out there is a role that will use all your gifts, match all your values, pay all your bills, and never make you question your life choices.

Call it the "dream job," "calling," "perfect fit," whatever.

We talk about it like it's a soulmate. The problem with the soulmate theory of work is that it makes every real, imperfect job look inferior. And it sets you up to stay too long in almost right spaces, waiting for them to become perfect if you just work hard enough. Here's a more grounded thought: most roles are temporary containers for your development. Some containers are obviously wrong from the start. Others are right for a season and then you quietly outgrow them. A few are spacious enough that you can keep evolving inside them for a long time.

But none of them were built to hold your entire lifetime of growth.

Once you accept that, moving your cheese stops feeling like a betrayal of destiny and starts feeling like routine upkeep. You're not leaving your "calling". You're leaving a container that can no longer hold it.

Let's look at the story of The Analyst Who Could See the Whole Board. Let's talk about Reggie. Reggie started as a data analyst at a mid-size tech company. He loved it at first. He got to dive into numbers, build dashboards, find patterns. His manager called him "a machine," which was somehow intended as a compliment. Over a few years, Reggie noticed something weird: he was more interested in the meetings after his slide deck than in the slides themselves. He wanted to stay in the room when leadership debated what to do with the data. He started seeing the whole chessboard, not just his square. He'd hand over his analysis and think, "We're solving the wrong problem," but his job description was clear: present numbers, answer questions, leave. He could have stayed in that loop forever: gather, analyze, present, repeat. The company would have been thrilled. He was fast, accurate, and uncomplaining. Instead, he started doing a risky thing: in one-on-one conversations, he'd offer a gentle, "Have we thought about it this way?" Sometimes people listened. Sometimes they didn't. One director pulled him aside and said, "You know, if you want to be part of these decisions, you need to stop acting like 'just the data guy.'" *That sentence stuck.*

Reggie realized the organization had him filed under "excellent contributor, not strategic." And he had cooperated in that classification because it was safe. People liked him in that box. A growth move for Reggie wasn't just applying for a new job. It was a deliberate identity shift: he began to show up as someone who not only reported on the game, but had a voice in how it was played.

That didn't fully fit where he was. **So he moved.**

He didn't leave because his job was bad. He left because his role in that system had become too small for who he knew he could be.

The Emotional Economics of Growth. There's a financial cost to moving your cheese. We talk about that a lot: salaries, benefits, relocation, risk. There's also an emotional economy at work that we rarely name. Every role, every organization, every relationship has its own emotional budget. There's how much disappointment you can tolerate, how much boredom, how much misalignment, how much silence. When you were younger in your career (or life), you were probably willing to pay a lot of emotional tax for the sake of learning, proving yourself, or just surviving. You swallowed things. You powered through. You told yourself it was temporary. As you grow, your emotional budget changes. You are less willing to spend your limited energy tolerating leaders who won't listen, missions that no longer make sense to you, or cultures that quietly punish honesty. You start to realize that every hour you spend managing your own resentment is an hour you're not spending doing work you actually care about. This isn't you becoming delicate. It's you realizing your emotional energy is a finite resource. Growth often looks like refusing to keep subsidizing systems that are too expensive for your sanity.

The Organizational Immune System. Here's a slightly uncomfortable metaphor: organizations have immune systems. When something new enters the body—an idea, a person, a way of working—the system responds. Sometimes it integrates the new thing, adapts, and gets stronger. Sometimes it treats the new thing as a threat and tries to neutralize it. When you start growing beyond your assigned role, you are, in a sense, a foreign object in the familiar system. *You might notice:*

You're left out of certain conversations you used to be in. Your suggestions are acknowledged but not acted on. You get labeled as "difficult" or "not a culture fit" the moment you stop nodding along.

Or, more subtly, people keep telling you, "You're so good in your lane," every time you try to step outside it. This doesn't mean the organization is evil. It means it's doing what systems do: maintain equilibrium. *Your growth is, by definition, a disturbance.* The deeper question becomes: is this a system that can metabolize your growth and get better because of it? Or is this a system that will only accept you as long as you remain in your previous form? If it's the latter, moving your cheese is not disloyalty. It's survival of your future self.

When You're the One Who Changed. We often frame growth moves as a reaction to something the organization did: they changed leadership, they shifted priorities, they became more political, less caring, more profit-driven, less human.

Sometimes that's true. Sometimes what changed was you.

You read books that made you think differently. You went to therapy and realized certain dynamics weren't okay. You got mentored by someone who raised your standards. You experienced a different culture where your voice mattered more. You led a side project and discovered you loved leading. Suddenly, things you used to tolerate feel corrosive. That meeting you used to shrug off as "just how it is" now leaves you buzzing with anger for hours. That comment your boss makes in front of others hits something in you that refuses to go back to sleep. That "joke" about your identity, your background, your boundaries doesn't slide by anymore. When that happens, it's tempting to either demonize the organization or gaslight yourself.

"This place is toxic." Or *"I'm being too sensitive."*

There is a third option: *"I outgrew what I used to accept."* That sentence is both humbling and empowering. It acknowledges that you participated in the old dynamic—and that you're no longer willing to. Growth doesn't always mean the place got worse. Sometimes it means your tolerance for what was already there got lower. And that's a sign of health.

Growth vs. Escapism: A Hard Self-Check. It's important to say this plainly: not every desire to move is growth. *Sometimes it's escapism in a blazer.*

If you find yourself wanting to change jobs, cities, or communities every time conflict arises, feedback hits a nerve, or boredom sets in, it's worth asking: "Am I moving forward, or just moving away?" One way to tell: imagine, for a moment, that leaving is off the table for the next six months. You're here. Period. What hard conversation would you need to have? What boundary would you need to set? What piece of feedback would you need to sit with instead of dismissing? What habit would you need to change? If you can't even entertain doing those things, there's a good chance you're using "growth" language to avoid necessary discomfort. Real growth often includes doing at least some of that internal work before you go, so you don't just pack your patterns in a box and unpack them at your next office. The goal is not to be perfect when you move—no one is—but to be honest about what you're running from and what you're running toward.

The Cost of Not Moving. We're very good at enumerating the risks of moving our cheese.

What if I fail?

What if I regret it?

What if I can't find something better?

What if people think I'm ungrateful?

We're less practiced at naming the risks of staying put when we know we've outgrown a place. What happens to your sense of agency if you repeatedly silence it? What happens to your creativity if you keep using it to decorate the cage instead of finding the door? What happens to your integrity if you keep co-signing decisions you no longer believe in? What happens to your relationships if the most honest parts of you never get airtime? There is a psychological toll to living out of alignment. *You might not explode. You erode.*

You become more cynical, less hopeful. More sarcastic, less sincere. You start making fun of the people who are still idealistic, not because they're wrong, but because you remember being like them and you don't like what you did with that version of yourself. Staying has a cost. It's just paid in installments small enough that no one sends you a bill. Until one day you look around and realize the person paying it has been you, for years.

The Quiet Work Before the Big Move. If this all sounds like a manifesto to quit your job tomorrow, it isn't. Growth moves can be decisive, but they're rarely reckless. Underneath every "sudden" exit that people gossip about, there were usually months (or years) of invisible shifts. The invisible work might look like:

- Admitting, privately, that you're done growing in your current role.

- Allowing yourself to be curious again about what you actually want, not just what's available on the job board.

- Noticing which meetings, topics, and projects wake you up, and which ones put you to sleep.

- Paying attention to who has the kind of life you quietly envy—not just the title, but the way they seem to inhabit themselves. You can do all of that without making a single announcement.

You're not betraying your organization by thinking about your life. In fact, some of the most responsible leaders are the ones who know when it's time to make room for someone else, instead of clinging to a role they've outgrown because it's familiar.

Practicing Being the Next Version of You. Before you move your cheese in a visible way, you can start practicing your next version inside your current environment. If the next version of you asks more strategic questions, you can start doing that now, in small, respectful ways. If the next version of you sets clearer boundaries, you can experiment with saying, "I can do this much by Friday; beyond that, I'd be over-committing." If the next version of you leads instead of just executes, you can own one small project end-to-end and treat it like a lab. Sometimes, just making those internal upgrades changes your experience enough that you don't need to move yet; the role stretches with you. Other times, it clarifies the fact that the space around you cannot or will not expand. Either way, you're not waiting for a new environment to "make you" different. You're becoming different on purpose and then choosing environments that can work with that.

When the Organization Can't Follow You. There's a kind of grief that comes when you realize your growth trajectory no longer fits inside the organization's trajectory, even if everyone has good intentions. You might be working for genuinely kind leaders who are limited by structures above them. You might be in a nonprofit that does meaningful work but can't offer you the stretch you need. You might be in a family business where every role you might step into would still have you playing the same emotional part you've played since childhood.

No one is the villain in those stories. And that almost makes it harder.

It would be easier if there were a clear bad guy to point at. "I left because of them" is very tidy. "I left because I changed and the system couldn't change with me" is harder to fit into a dinner-party anecdote. But it's closer to the truth for many people. Sometimes the bravest, most honest thing you can say is, "This is as far as we can go together." You honor what it was. You tell the truth about what it can't be. And you step into the unknown, not because you hate where you've been, but because you respect who you're becoming.

The Intelligence of the Itch. If you strip away the slogans and the self-help language, growth often starts as nothing more than an itch.

The itch to learn something that has nothing to do with your current job description.

The itch to speak up in a meeting where you've always stayed quiet.

The itch to stop laughing at jokes that aren't funny to you anymore.

The itch to say, "Actually, I don't agree," and see what happens.

It's easy to dismiss that itch as restlessness, immaturity, or entitlement. *Sometimes it is.* But sometimes that itch is the most intellectually honest part of you refusing to accept a life optimized for everyone else's comfort. You don't have to scratch it by blowing everything up. You can scratch it by asking better questions, having one braver conversation, taking one small action that aligns more with who you are now than who you were when you started. If that itch keeps coming back, if it grows more insistent every time you override it, it's not a phase. It's a message.

At some point, the cost of ignoring it will be higher than the cost of moving your cheese. You won't get a certificate when it's time. There is no "You May Now Grow" email. There is only you, in the middle of an ordinary Tuesday, realizing you've done everything you came here to do—and that staying any longer would be less about commitment and more about fear. You can thank the place. You can honor the people. You can acknowledge the version of you who really needed this chapter. And then, quietly, intelligently, with more self-respect than drama, you can start moving your cheese—not because everything is on fire, but because, for the first time, you're no longer willing to live on pilot light.

Sometimes, moving your cheese starts with moving your mindset, your schedule, or your next brave conversation. In the next chapter, we'll look at a more uncomfortable truth:

**Sometimes we don't move our cheese to survive or to grow.
Sometimes, we move it to hide.**

CHEESE CHECK

This chapter is about the moves you make not to survive, but to become. Give yourself room to dream and be honest.

Where in your life do you suspect you've outgrown the "pot"?

Work? Church? A role in your family? A city? A routine?

Finish the sentence: "This used to fit me, but lately I feel ___________."

What are your "restless gratitude" places?

List 2–3 areas where you are genuinely thankful and quietly unsettled. What might that restlessness be trying to tell you?

What "good thing" are you afraid to even imagine leaving?

Write it down, even if you're not ready to act. What story are you telling yourself about what it would mean if you left?

How do you tell the difference between growth and avoidance in yourself?

Think of a past move that was truly about growth. What did it feel like?

Think of a past move that was really about running. What did that feel like?

What are the warning signs you're about to repeat an avoidance pattern?

If you gave yourself permission to be a beginner again, what would you try?

A new field? A degree? A business? A creative project? A new way of serving?

Which one scares you and excites you at the same time?

Who, if anyone, might feel threatened by your growth—and how can you love them without shrinking?

Write a sentence you might say (or just say to yourself):

"I love you, and I'm still going to ___________."

What is one small, low-risk step toward growth you can take in the next 30 days?

A class, a conversation, an application, a visit, a research call, a savings plan? Write it down with a date. You don't have to blow up your life to honor your growth.

CHEESE CHECK NOTES

On the inside, you might be thinking:

"If i move fast enough, my unfinished business can't catch me."

The problem?

Unfinished business has good cardio.

It will jog right alongside you into the next season.

Dr. Laide R. Alexander

CHAPTER FIVE

I Moved to Hide My Cheese

Not every move is brave. Some moves look bold on the outside—new job, new city, new church, new relationship, new "season"—but if we're honest? *They're just new hiding places.*

You change your scenery. You change your circle. You change your title, your hair, your social media bio. But you don't change your patterns. You don't change your honesty. You don't change the parts of you that actually need to heal. And when the dust settles in the new place, you look around and realize: **"Somehow… I brought the same me with me."** It's not that the move was all bad. It's that the move wasn't all about what you said it was about underneath the "I'm just following my peace," "I am being shifted," and "I'm choosing me this year," there was a quieter sentence: ***I don't want to face this… so I'm leaving.*** This chapter is about those moves.

When "New" is Really Avoidance. Let's talk about some classic hiding moves. See if any sound familiar.

You leave a job… right when your performance review or a hard conversation is coming.

You leave a relationship… every time someone gets close enough to see your real fears.

You leave a church… every time leadership says "no" or holds you accountable.

You change cities… every time the loneliness you carry starts to feel too loud.

You start a "new project" … every time an old project reaches the boring, consistent part that requires discipline.

On the outside, you look adventurous: "They're always evolving!" "They're always onto the next thing!" On the inside, you might be thinking: "If I move fast enough, my unfinished business can't catch me." The problem? *Unfinished business has good cardio.* It will jog right alongside you into the next season.

The Stories We Tell So We Don't Have to Tell the Truth. Hiding moves often come wrapped in beautiful language. We say things like:

- "This place just isn't feeding me anymore."
- "My season here is up."
- "They're just not on my level spiritually."
- "I'm protecting my peace."
- "I deserve better energy around me."
- "God is calling me higher."

Sometimes those statements are true. Sometimes they are PR statements for "I don't want to do this hard work." *What hard work?* Apologizing, receiving correction, sitting in the discomfort of not being the favorite, admitting you dropped the ball, staying and growing through an awkward phase, letting people see that you don't always have it together, hiding moves let us keep our image clean at the cost of our character. We protect our reputation by abandoning our growth.

Are You Running From a Place or From a Mirror? Here's an uncomfortable question: "Am I running from them, or am I running from the mirror they are holding up to me?" Certain environments and relationships act like mirrors. They show you: Your impatience, your control issues, your insecurity, your jealousy, your need to be needed, your fear of not being special, your tendency to overpromise and underdeliver, and sometimes, instead of saying, "Wow, I don't like what I see in me," we say, "I don't like these people." *So we move.* We find a new job, a new church, a new partner, a new friend group where, at least for a while, no one knows our patterns yet. We get a grace period where we can still believe it was all them. The mirror didn't disappear. We just changed bathrooms.

When Boundaries Are Real and When They're Just Brick Walls.

Boundaries are healthy. We need them. But anything healthy can be misused. A real boundary sounds like:

- "I won't allow you to speak to me that way."

- "I can't take on that extra work."

- "I need to step back to take care of my health."

- "I'm not available for that kind of relationship."

A brick wall dressed up as a boundary sounds like:

- "I cut off anybody who…" (for things that could be talked through)

- "The moment someone disappoints me, I'm done."

- "I don't do hard conversations; that's just my boundary."

- "If you disagree with me, you're toxic."

In the name of "protecting our peace," we sometimes protect our immaturity. We leave every environment that challenges us and call it "self-care." Real boundaries make space for you to grow. Brick walls make sure you never have to.

The Pattern Test: What's the Common Denominator? If you're not sure whether a move was about growth, survival, or hiding, there's a simple test: Look for patterns. Do most of your jobs end the same way? Do most of your relationships end with the same script? Do you have a trail of "they just didn't appreciate me" behind you? Does every church eventually become "not deep enough / too controlling / not affirming enough / too messy" in the exact same way? Does every business, ministry, or creative project die right after the exciting beginning? If the story is always:

- "They weren't ready for someone like me."

- "People are intimidated by my calling."

- "Folks are just too fake."

…but the cast keeps changing and you're always the main character…It might be time to ask: "What part of this story am I bringing with me every time?"

That question is not about blame. It's about power. Because *if you're the common denominator, you're also the common opportunity.*

When You Hide Behind "Purpose" and "Calling". One of the easiest places to hide is behind spiritual language. We say: "My season here is over; God is elevating me." "God is shifting me into a new assignment." They just don't understand my anointing." Meanwhile, the real story is: *You were asked to be on time. You were told "no" to something you wanted. You were given feedback you didn't like. You were asked to submit to process instead of skipping steps.* So instead of sitting with the discomfort, you turn it into a calling story.

The scary part? People will often applaud your hiding if you package it in the right religious wrapping. But deep down, you know the difference between: "God is truly stretching me into a new thing," and "I'm running before they see I don't want to be stretched at all." God is not fragile. You don't have to use God as a cover story for your avoidance.

The Cost of Constant Relocation. Moving your cheese to hide feels like relief at first. No more awkward meetings. No more hard talks. No more accountability. No more "Can we talk about what happened?" You get a hit of fresh air. But constant relocation has a cost: You never build roots. Relationships stay shallow. Communities stay temporary. You never see the long-term fruit of your own growth. You leave right before you would've seen what staying and changing could do. You train yourself to escape, not to transform. *The muscle* *that gets strong is not "courage" or "integrity." It's "run."* Here's a hard truth: If you always leave when it gets real, you will never know what you're like when you stay and grow. You deserve to meet the version of you who doesn't just start well but stays well when it matters.

When Staying Is Actually the Braver Move. Sometimes, the bravest thing you can do is not to move your cheese at all. It's to:

- Stay in the job long enough to own your mistakes and improve.

- Stay in the friendship long enough to have a hard conversation.

- Stay in church long enough to work through conflict instead of ghosting.

- Stay in therapy long enough to hit the part where you don't like what you're hearing.

Staying is not always the answer. But reflexively leaving is not always "self-care." Before you move, ask yourself: "Is there a conversation I'm avoiding?" "Is there an apology I owe?" "Is there feedback I haven't really sat with?" "If this exact same issue followed me to the next place, would I still think it was all them?" If leaving means you never have to ask those questions, you might be hiding.

Compassion for the Part of You That Hides. Before you start beating yourself up, let's pause. The part of you that hides is not evil. It's protective. That part of you learned, somewhere, that: Being wrong is dangerous. Being seen is unsafe. Being vulnerable gets you hurt. Being honest gets you abandoned. Being still means getting stuck. *So it learned to move. Quickly.* It said: "We will not be embarrassed. We will not be left. We will not be small. We will leave first." *That part of you deserves compassion, not condemnation.* You can say to it:

- "Thank you for trying to keep me safe.

- You helped me survive some things.

But we're not in that same danger anymore. We can try a different way now." Growth is not about firing your survival strategies with shame. It's about gently retraining them.

Bringing Your Cheese Out of Hiding. So what does it look like to stop moving your cheese to hide? It might look like: Staying put long enough to finish something you start. Choosing one community and practicing honesty there. Letting someone see you in process, not just in victory. Owning, "I left because I was scared," instead of inventing a more noble story. Going back—not always physically, but emotionally—to clean up what you ran from where it's safe and appropriate. It might also look like telling the full truth about past moves: "I said it was about them. The truth is, I was also avoiding my own stuff." That kind of honesty feels like taking off armor in public. But it's also how you stop dragging the same unhealed patterns from maze to maze.

You can move your cheese for all kinds of reasons.

To survive.

To grow.

To explore.

And then there's this other category we don't like to talk about: You moved your cheese to hide. You packed your boxes, updated your LinkedIn, changed your number, found a new church, joined a new team, maybe even got a new therapist. On the outside, it looked bold. "Wow, look at them stepping into a new season." "So brave." "So obedient to the 'next thing.'" On the inside, if you're very honest, a quieter sentence was driving the U-Haul:

"I really don't want to deal with this... so I'm leaving."

This chapter is about those moves. Not to shame them. To name them. Because you can't change a pattern you're still calling by the wrong name.

New Job, Same You. You know that first week in a new job? The badge is shiny. The welcome swag is still in the box. You're learning names, acronyms, where the decent coffee is. People are friendly. No one has strong opinions about you yet. It's a beautiful, brief season of being "the new person" instead of "the person with a history." For a while, the novelty works like anesthesia.

Then, slowly, the numbness wears off. One day you catch yourself in a meeting, feeling the exact same irritation, the exact same defensiveness, the exact same urge to shut down that you felt in your old job. Different logos. Same reaction. You notice you're doing that again:

Smiling and saying, "No worries!" while mentally compiling a list of every slight.

Saying "It's fine" when it's not, then resenting people for not reading your mind.

Overpromising in the name of being impressive, then burning out so you don't have to admit you overpromised.

You moved teams. You moved companies. You moved industries. And somehow, you brought the same emotional choreography with you. The geography changed. The cast changed.

The script… did not. That's the essence of moving your cheese to hide: the scenery updates so you don't have to.

The Performance Review Escape Hatch. Let's start with a very corporate version of hiding, because it's common and socially acceptable. You've been at your job a couple of years. The honeymoon is over. People have seen both your strengths and your "areas of opportunity" (that's HR for "things we're tired of talking to you about"). You know a serious performance conversation is coming. Maybe your manager has dropped hints. Maybe you've missed some key deliverables. Maybe your attitude has been… noticeable. Right on cue, you get very spiritual or very visionary.

You start saying things like:

"I just feel like my season here is ending."

"I don't feel aligned with the culture anymore."

"I think the Lord is shifting me."

"I'm just not being challenged."

Are any of those possibly true? Sure. But if we zoom in, the timeline looks suspicious: Feedback is coming. Instead of sitting in the discomfort, you suddenly feel "called elsewhere." You resign just before the hard conversation hits paper. From the outside, it looks like a decisive move. From the inside, it's a well-timed exit to avoid hearing, in plain language, how your behavior is impacting other people.

You didn't just move your cheese. You moved your accountability.

Let me tell you the story of: The High Performer Who Hated Being Average

Let's call her, Amber. In every environment she'd ever been in, Amber was the star. Top of her class, youngest manager in her previous company, the one people said, "We don't know what we'd do without you." She took a new role at a larger, more complex organization. Bigger stage. More opportunity. Also: more people at her level who were just as smart, just as driven, just as capable. For the first six months, she loved it. New challenges. New systems. New lingo. Then the first performance cycle came around. Her review was… good. Not bad. Not glowing. Solid. "Meets expectations." She wanted to throw the document across the room. Meets expectations? Amber had built an entire identity on "exceeds." She didn't know how to metabolize "fine." Her manager offered thoughtful feedback: places she could grow, blind spots, ways she was rubbing peers the wrong way. It wasn't cruel. It was accurate.

Two weeks later, Amber announced, "I just don't feel seen here. I'm going to take some time to figure out my next calling." If you listened to her tell the story, it sounded like a values conflict. "They just didn't recognize my leadership." "They weren't ready for someone like me." "I need to be in a place that celebrates excellence." If you listened closely, you could hear the subtext:

"I don't know who I am if I'm not the favorite. I'd rather leave than stay and grow through being normal for a while." **Amber moved her cheese.** She did not move her relationship with being average long enough to become excellent again at a new level.

When "New" Is Just Better Wallpaper. We live in a culture that worships the fresh start. New job. New city. New team. New startup. New "brand." New congregation. New partner. New therapist. New gym. New planner. There's a rush in that. A feeling of, "This time it'll be different." And sometimes, it is. But sometimes, all we've done is change the wallpaper on the same room. You leave a job a month before the big project launches, right when it would require consistency instead of adrenaline. You leave a relationship as soon as the honeymoon fades and the real work of intimacy begins. You leave a church when you're asked to move from "being fed" to actually serving. You leave a city when you realize that your loneliness followed you there. From the outside, you look like a dynamic, evolving person. "They're always reinventing themselves." "They're not afraid of change." From the inside, if you dare to be honest, you might think: "If I move fast enough, the parts of me I don't want to see can't catch up."

Spoiler: they can. Unfinished business has elite endurance. It will jog right alongside your "new chapter," waiting for you to notice that it didn't die just because your area code changed.

Rebranding Avoidance as Growth. One of the most sophisticated forms of hiding is language. We are brilliant at giving noble names to our fears. "I'm protecting my peace" can mean you've finally learned to set boundaries. It can also mean you've decided any conversation that makes you uncomfortable is "toxic." "I'm choosing me this year" can mean you're honoring your needs. It can also mean you're done apologizing, even when you're wrong. "I'm just not being fed here" might be a real lack of development. It might also be that you were asked to show up on time, follow process, or receive correction, and you didn't like how that felt. There's nothing wrong with wanting peace, or protection, or development. The problem is when those words become a PR strategy to keep you from having to say the less glamorous sentence:

"I don't want to look at my part in this." We are so practiced at spinning a narrative that sometimes we believe our own press releases. We tell the elegant version of why we left a job, a church, a friendship, a project so often that we forget the unedited draft that never made it to LinkedIn. Growth begins where the press release ends.

Mirrors in Work Clothes. Here's an unsettling question to sit with:

"Am I running from this place… or from the version of me this place is showing me?"

Certain environments function like mirrors. Not because they're perfect, but because they're revealing.

A blunt manager is a mirror for your sensitivity to criticism.

A structured organization is a mirror for your resistance to process.

A high-performing team is a mirror for your relationship with being outshone.

A healthy partner is a mirror for your discomfort with being fully seen.

You don't have to like everything you see in those mirrors. But if your first instinct, every time a mirror appears, is to smash it and walk out of the room, you're not escaping toxic people; you're escaping your own reflection. It's much easier to say, "They're so controlling," than to say, "I don't like that I still need constant praise to feel okay." It's easier to say, "They just don't recognize my gift," than to say, "I overpromise because I'm afraid that steady, normal contribution won't be enough."

It's easier to say, "This place is full of fake people," than to say, "I don't like that I become fake here to be liked." Sometimes the place is a problem. Not every mirror is accurate. Some are warped. But if every place eventually becomes "the problem," and you never stay long enough to see a different version of yourself emerge, the common factor isn't them. It's the part of you that chooses where to stand when the mirror gets too clear.

Let me tell you a story about: *The Serial Quitter in a Blazer.*

Meet Tope. On paper, Tope looked fearless. By 35, he'd worked in four cities, five companies, three industries. Every jump came with a good story.

"This place wasn't innovative enough."

"That leadership team was threatened by my ideas."

"That church wasn't serious about justice."

"That startup wasn't ready for my level of excellence."

There was some truth in all of those assessments. None of the places he left were perfect. But if you looked closely, the exits had a pattern. Each time, right before he left:

Someone confronted him about being chronically late on deliverables.

A colleague finally told him, "You don't listen; you just wait to talk."

A leader asked him to stay focused on one project instead of pitching five new ones.

A friend gently mentioned that every disagreement with him turned into a referendum on their loyalty.

Within weeks of those moments, Tope would feel "led" to move on. "I just don't feel valued here," he'd say. And he believed it. In his fifth job, a mentor pulled him aside and said, "Hey. I love your drive. But have you noticed you always leave right after someone calls you on something?" Tope laughed it off. Then went home, shut the door, and cried. He realized he had built a life that allowed him to keep his self-image intact by never staying in one place long enough for anyone to see past it. He wasn't moving to new opportunities. He was moving to keep his reflection flattering.

Boundaries or Brick Walls? Let's talk about boundaries. Boundaries are good. Necessary. Healthy. In organizations, they sound like:

"I'm not available after 7 p.m. unless it's an emergency."

"I can't take on that extra project without dropping something else."

"I'm not comfortable being spoken to like that in a meeting."

Boundaries protect your time, your energy, your dignity. Brick walls, on the other hand, protect your ego. Brick walls sound like:

"The moment someone disappoints me, I'm done."

"I don't do hard conversations; that's just my boundary."

"If you disagree with me, you're negative and I can't be around that energy."

On social media, brick walls get sold as self-care. "Cut people off at the first sign of…" fill in the blank. In real life, brick walls make sure you never have to tolerate the discomfort of being confronted, challenged, or disagreed with. In the workplace, you can see this when an employee says, "I need psychological safety," and what they mean is, "I need to never hear anything that makes me feel bad about myself." Psychological safety is about being able to take interpersonal risks without fear of humiliation or punishment. It is not about being shielded from every feeling of embarrassment, frustration, or defensiveness. The question isn't "Do I have boundaries?" The question is, "Are my boundaries helping me grow—or just helping me hide?"

The Pattern Behind the Stories. If you're wondering whether a past move was about growth, survival, or hiding, one way to tell is to zoom out. Not from that one story, but from your life. How do your jobs tend to end? How do your friendships tend to end? How do your church experiences, your collaborations, your projects tend to end? Is there a recurring scene? Do you often leave right after conflict appears? Right after feedback is given? Right after the "fun, visionary" phase ends and the "boring, consistent" phase begins? Right after someone asks you to be more specific, more accountable, more present? If every job eventually becomes "They just didn't appreciate me," every community becomes "They were fake," every leader becomes "intimidated by my calling or skills," but the names and faces keep changing while your role in the story stays suspiciously similar…that's not an indictment. *It's an invitation.*

Because if you're the common denominator, you're also the common opportunity. You are the only variable you always have access to change.

Hiding Behind "Calling" and "Purpose". There's a special category of hiding that thrives in purpose-driven environments—churches, nonprofits, mission-oriented companies. In those spaces, we have a whole vocabulary that can be used to cloak simple avoidance.

"My season here is over."

"I'm being shifted into a new assignment."

"They just don't understand my gift."

"I'm called to higher."

Sometimes that's real. Seasons do end. Callings do shift. But sometimes the real story is embarrassingly ordinary:

You were asked to be on time.

You were told, "No, not yet."

You were given feedback you didn't like.

You were asked to submit to a process instead of skipping steps.

You were reminded that other people's needs matter too.

Instead of sitting with the discomfort of that, you wrote a spiritual press release. The scary part? People will often applaud this.

If you frame your exit as "stepping into purpose" or "answering God's call," few folks will say, "Are you sure you're not just avoiding growth?"

They'll throw you a farewell party. You'll get a video montage. You'll leave with your image intact. But you'll also leave with your unresolved relationship to structure, feedback, and shared responsibility. God is not fragile. Purpose is not so delicate that it needs to be protected from honest self-examination. You are allowed to say, "I think I used calling language to justify leaving a situation that was exposing parts of me I didn't want to see."

That honesty doesn't disqualify you. It qualifies you to actually grow into the purpose you keep tweeting about.

The Cost of Constant Relocation. Moving your cheese to hide feels good at first. Relief. Space. No more awkward debriefs. No more "Can we talk?" calendar invites. No more sitting in a room where people know what you did last quarter.

You get to start fresh. You get that "clean slate" high. But there are long-term costs to making escape your primary coping skill. You never build roots. You never stay long enough to see yourself change in public. You never experience the strange, deep satisfaction of repairing something you helped break. You never get to see what your leadership looks like after people have watched you own your mess and grow.

Every environment stays shallow.

Every community stays temporary.

Every story ends at the same chapter: "And then I left."

The muscle that gets strong is not courage. It's sprinting. You become very good at beginnings and very poor at middles. You deserve to meet the version of you who can do both.

Let me tell you the story about: *The Team That Never Kept a Leader*

There was a department in a mid-sized company—we'll call it Customer Solutions—that had a reputation: they "couldn't keep good leaders." Every 18 months, a new manager would arrive, full of ideas and energy, and within a year and a half, they'd be gone. The story in the company was, "That team is cursed." "Those people are impossible." "Leadership burnout is just part of the role." One year, a new director, Lila, took over. She was competent, warm, a little nerdy about processes. For the first six months, things were rocky, as expected. New expectations. New systems. New ways of doing things. Around month seven, she started having one-on-ones about performance and behavior.

Not in a punitive way. Just… direct. "Hey, I've noticed you're always five to ten minutes late to calls. What's going on?" "I'm seeing that you miss deadlines and then go quiet. How can we handle that differently?" "When you vent in the group chat, it affects the whole team vibe. Let's talk about how to raise concerns constructively." Within three months, three of the longest-tenured team members resigned. Their exit narratives were almost identical:

"This place just isn't what it used to be."

"I don't feel valued."

"I don't feel like leadership trusts me."

"I'm protecting my peace."

Lila was rattled. Had she been too harsh? Had she missed something? She pulled in HR. She pulled in her own mentor. She asked, "Am I out of line?" The answer, from people who had watched a decade of churn, was sobering:

"You're the first leader who hasn't tried to win them over with perks or avoid the hard stuff. You're the first one to calmly ask them to grow. They've never had to do that here. Every time someone has gotten close to naming their patterns, those employees have left—and the leader has been blamed."

For years, the story had been, "We can't keep good leaders." The truer story was, "We can't keep people who hold up mirrors." The team wasn't cursed. They had just learned that if they made it uncomfortable enough, any leader who challenged them would eventually give up and go away. *Mary didn't.*

Over time, the team changed. New people came in. Some old ones stayed and did the hard work. The department's reputation slowly shifted from "drama" to "solid." But only because someone finally refused to move their cheese just to hide from the conflict.

When Staying Is Actually Braver. In a book about moving cheese, it might sound strange to say this, but it needs to be said:

Sometimes the bravest, most growth-producing thing you can do is not to move your cheese at all. **It is to stay.**

To stay in the job long enough to hear the full version of your performance review and not immediately update your résumé. To stay in the friendship long enough to say, "It hurt me when…" and listen to the answer. To stay in the team long enough to bring up the tension instead of ghosting emotionally. To stay in therapy long enough to hit the layer where you don't like what you're hearing and not fire your therapist. Staying is not always the answer. Some situations are truly unsafe, unhealthy, or misaligned. But if your default setting is "I leave when it gets real," it might be time to experiment with the opposite. Before you pack, ask:

Is there a conversation I'm avoiding?

Is there an apology I owe?

Is there feedback I haven't really digested?

If this exact issue followed me to the next place (and it will), would I handle it any differently there?

If leaving means you never have to find out, you might not be moving on. *You might be hiding.*

Compassion for the Hider. Now, before you start drafting a 12-page self-indictment, let's slow down. The part of you that hides is not evil. It's protective. At some point in your story, it likely learned very convincing lessons:

Being wrong is dangerous.

Being seen is unsafe.

Being vulnerable gets you hurt.

Being honest gets you punished or abandoned.

Staying still means getting stuck in something you can't survive. So that part of you got very good at one thing: leaving first. "We will not be embarrassed. We will not be surprised. We will not let them see us sweat. We will go before they can reject, expose, or confine us." That strategy may have saved you, once. Maybe you did need to run from a truly harmful environment. Maybe you did need to reinvent yourself to escape an identity that was killing you. Maybe you did need to move cities, careers, communities to get a shot at a different life.

Honor that. Then, gently, notice where that same strategy is now over-firing. You can talk to that part of you—the runner, the hider—with some kindness:

"Thank you. You helped us get out of real danger. You're good at moving. But not every discomfort is the same kind of danger. We're older now. We have more tools. We don't have to leave every time something feels hard."

Growth is not about firing your survival strategies with shame. It's about retraining them for a world where you're not always under threat.

Bringing Your Cheese Out of Hiding. So what does it look like, practically, to stop moving your cheese to hide? It will look different for everyone, but there are some common moves:

You stay put long enough to finish something you start, even when the dopamine wears off. You choose one community—a team, a group of friends, a professional circle—and practice being honest there, not just impressive. You let at least one person see you in process instead of only after the victory lap.

You tell the truth—to yourself first—about past moves:

"I said I left because they didn't value me. The truth is, I also didn't want to face how I was showing up." "I blamed the culture, and yes, there were issues. But I also ghosted instead of having the hard conversation."

You go back, where it's safe and appropriate—not always physically, but emotionally—to clean up what you can. That might be an email: "I've had time to reflect, and I realize I owe you an apology for how I left." It might be a conversation: "I told myself a story about you that wasn't fair. Here's what I've learned." You don't do this to grovel. You do it to prove to yourself that you are capable of something other than running. You start making decisions based on who you want to become, not just what you want to escape. And slowly, your life shifts. Your moves stop being elaborate hiding strategies. They become what they were always meant to be: conscious, aligned, sometimes scary, often messy, but rooted in truth. Because you can't build a new life on top of an old lie. You can only stack so many fresh starts on a foundation of "It was all them" before the whole structure starts to feel wobbly. Pull the lie out. Tell the deeper truth. "Yes, there were real issues there. And yes, I was also avoiding my own." That sentence is heavier than "new season, who dis?" It's also strong enough to hold the weight of a life where you don't have to keep sprinting from maze to maze, hoping the next one will finally let you keep your cheese in peace.

You may still move. You may still change jobs, cities, roles, communities. But you'll know, in your bones, that this time, you're not just hiding your cheese. You're choosing where to place it—with your eyes open.

You can't build a new life on top of an old lie.

CHEESE CHECK

This chapter is not about shaming you. It's about freeing you. Be as honest as you can; no one else has to see this.

Name one move that, if you're honest, was at least partly about hiding.

"I left _____________________________, and underneath my reasons, I was really avoiding _________________."

What hard thing were you trying not to face in that situation?

Correction? Apology? Exposure? Boredom? Responsibility? Commitment? Write it in one clear sentence.

What story did you tell others about that move?

How much of it was true? How much of it was "PR" to protect your image?

Look for patterns. Do you see a repeated way your jobs, churches, relationships, or projects tend to end? What's the common denominator in those endings?

Where might you be using "boundaries" or "protecting my peace" to avoid growth?

Write 1–2 examples where you cut someone or something off quickly. Ask yourself: *"Was there a conversation or lesson I skipped?"*

Talk to the part of you that hides.

Write a short note to that part:

"I know you're trying to protect me from __________. Thank you.

From now on, we're going to try __________ instead of always running."

Is there one place in your current life where you're tempted to run right now? Job, church, relationship, project, city?

Before you move, what one honest conversation or action could you take here first?

Remember: You don't have to stay in every situation. Some places truly are unhealthy. But if you always move your cheese to avoid being seen, stretched, or accountable, you will keep meeting the same test in a new room. You are capable of more than running.

In the next chapter, we'll look at a quieter pattern that can be just as powerful as survival, growth, or hiding: The times when you didn't really move your cheese at all…You just let other people move it for you.

CHEESE CHECK NOTES

Taking back your agency is not a betrayal of your history.

It's a continuation of your healing.

Dr. Laide R. Alexander

CHAPTER SIX

I Let Other People Move My Cheese

Not every story is, "I moved my cheese to survive," or "I moved my cheese to grow," or even "I moved my cheese to hide." Sometimes the story is quieter:

- "I didn't really move my cheese at all.

- I just… let other people move it for me."

You didn't slam any doors. You didn't make any big speeches. You didn't pack up in the middle of the night. You just: Went along. Nodded. Signed. Showed up. Smiled for the photo. Swallowed your "no." And watched your own life be rearranged around you. From the outside, you look agreeable, flexible, and easygoing. On the inside, a small voice is whispering: *I never actually chose this.* This chapter is for the people who have spent more time adjusting to decisions than making them.

When "Easygoing" Becomes "Absent". There is nothing wrong with being laid-back. The world needs people who: Don't have to control everything. Can adapt when plans change. Aren't rigid or demanding. But there is a difference between: "I'm flexible," and "I'm missing from my own life." You might recognize this if: You regularly say, "I don't care, whatever works," even when you do care. People describe you as "so easy," but inside you feel unseen. Major life choices—jobs, moves, ministries, even relationships—seem to "just happen" to you. You look up one day and realize you are living a life that fits everyone's expectations but your own. At first, being easygoing gets you praise:

- "You're such a team player."

- "You're so low-maintenance."

- "You're always there when we need you."

But over time, it can cost you something vital: Your sense of agency—that quiet inner knowing that says, "I get a say in what happens to me."

How We Learn to Hand Over Our Cheese. Nobody wakes up and says, "Please, somebody else run my life." We learn to hand over our cheese. Maybe you learned:

- In a family where speaking up was punished or ignored

- In a culture or church that equated obedience with silence

- In relationships where love felt conditional on you not making waves

- In workplaces where pushing back meant being labeled "difficult," "angry," or "ungrateful"

So you adapted. You thought:

- "It's safer if I just go along."

- "It's easier if I let them decide."

"At least if it goes wrong, I can say it wasn't my idea." Over time, you may even start to believe: "I'm just not a decisive person." "I'm not a leader." "I'm not good at knowing what I want." But often, the truth is simpler and more tender: "I haven't had many safe places to practice wanting."

The Hidden Benefits of Not Choosing. Let's be honest: there are perks to letting other people move your cheese. When you don't choose, you can: Avoid conflict. Avoid disappointing people. Avoid being blamed if things go badly. Avoid the anxiety of making the "wrong" decision. Keep your image as the "good one," the "loyal one," the "supportive one" You get to say:

- "I was just doing what they asked."

- "It wasn't really my call."

"I'm just here to help."

Sometimes, those statements are true. But if that's your whole life story, something important is missing. ***You.***

Because while you are avoiding blame, you are also avoiding ownership. And without ownership, you can't fully experience: Deep satisfaction, real alignment with your values, and the joy (and weight) of living a life that actually fits you.

The Quiet Resentment of a Passive Life. Here's the twist: Even when you let other people move your cheese, your heart still keeps score. You might notice:

- A low-grade resentment toward your spouse, boss, pastor, or family

- A vague sense of having been "robbed," even if no one did anything obviously wrong

- Moments where you explode over something small because you've been quietly saying "yes" for too long

You might think: "They never consider me." "They just assume I'll adjust." "No one ever asks what I want." Sometimes that's accurate. But sometimes, if we're honest, we never gave them a real "no" to work with. We trained people to believe: "I'm fine with whatever." "I'll make it work." "I don't have needs, goals, or preferences that would ever disrupt the plan."

Resentment is what grows in the gap between what you say and what you actually want. The solution is not to become selfish. The solution is to become honest.

The Fear Behind "I Don't Know What I Want". Many people will say, "I don't know what I want." Sometimes that's true. Many times, it's not the whole story. Often, it means:

- "I've never been allowed to ask that question."

- "I'm afraid that if I say what I want, I'll lose love, safety, or approval."

- "I'm scared that what I want is impossible or will require too much change."

- "If I admit what I want, I'll have to face how far my current life is from that."

So "I don't know" becomes a kind of emotional bubble wrap. It protects you from: Hope. Disappointment. Responsibility

But it also protects you from: Fulfillment. Joy. Authenticity.

What if "I don't know what I want" became, "I'm learning to admit what I want, even if it scares me"?

Difference Between Surrender and Disappearance. If you are a person of faith, you've probably heard language like: "Not my will, but Yours be done." "Die to yourself." "Deny yourself." These are powerful, sacred ideas—when understood correctly. But many of us heard:

- "God's will = I never want anything."

- "Holiness = I disappear."

- "Maturity = I let everyone else go first, always."

There is a big difference between: Surrender, which is: "I bring my real desires to God and hold them with open hands," and Disappearance, which is: "I pretend I don't have desires so no one can ever accuse me of being selfish." Surrender requires a self to bring. Disappearance erases the self entirely. God is not honored by you being a ghost in your own life.

Small Ways You Hand Over the Pen. Let's bring this down to earth. You might be letting others move your cheese when you:

- Let your boss keep adding "just one more thing" to your plate because you never say, "This is too much."

- Let your family decide every holiday plan, even when you're exhausted, and say, "It's fine, I'll adjust."

- Let your partner decide all the financial, parenting, or life decisions while you "trust" them—but also quietly resent them.

Let your church, culture, or community dictate every life milestone, and you never ask, "Is this actually what I feel called to?"

Each choice might seem small. But over years, they add up to a life you didn't really co-author. You don't have to grab the pen and write every line alone. But you do get to hold your part of the story.

Practicing a Different Kind of "Yes" and "No". If you've spent years defaulting to other people, changing overnight is unrealistic—and unnecessary. You can start small. A healthy yes sounds like:

- "I want to do this."
- "I can do this without betraying myself."
- "I've checked in with my limits, and this fits."

A healthy no sounds like:

- "I can't take that on right now."
- "That doesn't work for me."
- "I need to think about it before I commit."
- "I'm not comfortable with that."

At first, using these sentences may feel: Rude. Selfish. Awkward. Terrifying. That's normal. You're building a new muscle. People who have been used to your automatic "yes" may push back:

- "What's wrong with you lately?"
- "You've changed."
- "You're being difficult."

You can quietly think: "Yes, I've changed. I've started showing up in my own life."

When Others Really Did Move Your Cheese. We also need to honor this: Sometimes, you didn't just "let" others move your cheese. They moved it through: Abuse, neglect, manipulation, abandonment, systemic injustice, decisions you truly had not power to influence. If that's your story, this isn't about blaming you for what was done to you. It is about asking: "Given what they did, how can I begin to reclaim some say in what happens next?"

That might look like:

- Getting help (therapy, pastoral care, support groups) to untangle the pattern

- Learning to trust your own voice again

- Letting yourself want things that were once off-limits

- Making one small decision entirely for you, without asking permission

Taking back your agency is not a betrayal of your history. It's a continuation of your healing.

You Are Allowed to Be a Co-Author: Here's the shift this chapter is inviting: From: *"Life happens to me; I just respond."* to *"Life happens, and I participate."* You are not the only author of your story. Many hands have written on your pages. But you are allowed to pick up the pen. You are allowed to say:

- "I don't want to do that anymore."

- "That used to fit me; it doesn't now."

- "I hear what you want. Here's what I want."

- "I need time to think about this decision."

- "I'm grateful for your input, and I'm still going to choose this."

This doesn't mean you never compromise. It means you stop disappearing as the price of peace.

Real peace can hold honest, present people. You can live an entire decade of your life without ever technically "moving your cheese" and still wake up one day feeling like you're in the wrong maze.

Not because you ran. Not because you hid. But because you quietly let other people drag your cheese from corner to corner while you smiled, nodded, and said, "Whatever works." From the outside, you look flexible. Adaptable.

Low-maintenance. A dream to work with. A solid partner. A steady friend. From the inside, something smaller and more honest is whispering:

"I never actually chose this."

This chapter is about that whisper. Not the dramatic exits. Not the bold new chapters. The quieter story so many smart, kind, responsible people live:

"I didn't really move my cheese. I just kept adjusting while other people moved it around me."

How a Life Gets Rearranged Without Your Consent Form.

Lives rarely get hijacked in one big moment. It's more like a series of tiny, reasonable adjustments.

You take the job your mentor thinks is perfect for you.

You stay in the city your family prefers.

You accept the promotion your boss insists you'd be "crazy to turn down."

You join the ministry, the committee, the project because "you'd be so good at it."

You agree to the timeline your partner wants for marriage, kids, houses, moves.

None of those decisions, on their own, feel like a betrayal. Each one has a good reason. A story that makes sense. A spreadsheet. A prayer. A pros-and-cons list. But at some point, if you zoom out, you realize that most of your major moves were heavily influenced—or outright scripted—by other people's preferences, fears, and expectations. You've been a responsible character in everyone else's story. *Your own storyline is… fuzzy.*

"Easygoing" vs. Missing. Let's be clear: there is nothing wrong with being easygoing. Organizations and families need people who can flex. Every team has at least one person whose superpower is "It's fine, we'll figure it out." These people keep planes from being burned down over seating assignments and projects from imploding when the plan inevitably shifts.

But there's a line between "I'm flexible" and "I'm not really here."

You cross that line when:

You say, "I don't care, whatever works," so often that people stop believing you ever have a preference.

You're the default "yes" for every gap, every extra task, every family obligation, because "you never complain."

The big pillars of your life—career, location, community, schedule—feel like they "just kind of happened," even though your name is on all the paperwork. At first, this gets you praised.

"You're such a team player."

"You're so low-maintenance."

"You're always there when we need you."

Over time, you feel a strange hollowness when people say those things. Because what they're really praising is how little space you take up.

Let me tell you a story: *The Promotion She Never Really Wanted*

Take Penelope. Penelope worked at a large healthcare organization. She was competent, kind, and very good at smoothing chaos. When her manager left, leadership pulled her into a meeting. "We'd love for you to step into the role," they said. "You already know the team. Everyone trusts you. It's the logical next step."

Penelope's internal reaction was… complicated. On one hand, this was the obvious promotion track. More money. More influence. The LinkedIn announcement would be a hit. Her parents would be proud. On the other hand, she knew what that job looked like up close: constant politics, endless meetings, very little of the patient-facing work she actually enjoyed. She heard herself say, "Wow, I'm honored. Let me think about it."

What she wanted to say was, "I don't think this is for me. I'd rather deepen my current role or explore a different path." She went home and asked a few people for advice.

Her mom: "You can't turn that down. Women don't get these chances all the time."

Her mentor: "This is exactly what we've been working toward. Don't self-sabotage."

Her colleagues: "You'd be so good. And if someone else gets it, who knows what they'll be like."

No one said, "Do you want it?"

Penelope eventually said yes. She did a good job. She adjusted. She learned the politics. She played the part. Two years later, sitting in yet another budget meeting, she thought, "I never actually chose this for me. I chose it so other people wouldn't be disappointed." The organization had moved her cheese into a corner labeled "Leadership Pipeline." She had never truly decided to live there.

How We Learn to Hand Over the Cheese. Very few people wake up at 18 and say, "My dream is to let other people make all my important decisions."

We learn it. Maybe you grew up in a family where speaking up was either ignored or punished. Where expressing a preference was labeled "selfish," where questioning an adult was "disrespectful," where the easiest way to keep the peace was to shrink. Maybe you were in a social or religious environment where obedience was equated with silence. Where "submission" meant never disagreeing. Where "honor" meant never saying, "This doesn't work for me." Maybe your early relationships taught you that love was conditional. As long as you were easy, agreeable, undemanding, you were cherished. The moment you had a boundary, a request, or a need, the temperature in the room changed. Maybe your first workplace made it painfully clear that people who pushed back were labeled "difficult," "ungrateful," or "not a culture fit."

You're smart. You adapted. You learned that the safest role to play was "I'll adjust." And because you got rewarded for it—approval, harmony, less conflict—that role slowly became your personality.

"I'm just not decisive."

"I'm easy."

"I'm chill."

"I'm here to serve."

Sometimes that's true. Often it's camouflage. Underneath there's a quieter, more vulnerable sentence:

"I haven't had many safe places to practice wanting."

The Hidden Perks of Not Choosing. Let's be honest: there are benefits to letting other people move your cheese. When you don't choose, you get to:

Avoid conflict. No one can be mad at you for a decision you never really made.

Avoid direct blame. If it goes badly, you can say, "Well, it wasn't my call."

Avoid the anxiety of picking "wrong." You never have to live with the fear that your decision ruined everything.

Maintain your role as "the good one." The loyal one. The servant. The helper. The supportive spouse, employee, child, congregant.

You get to say lines like:

"I was just doing what they asked."

"I'm just here to help."

"I trust their judgment."

Sometimes that's accurate and healthy. But if that becomes your whole strategy for life, something crucial is missing: ***You.***

Because while you're avoiding blame, you're also avoiding ownership. Without ownership, you might be safe—but you're not really alive. You won't feel the full weight of failure, but you also won't feel the deep satisfaction of building something that actually reflects you.

The Quiet Resentment That Builds in the Background. Here's the twist no one tells you when they praise you for being "so easy":

Your nervous system is keeping the receipts. Even if you say, "I don't care" out loud, somewhere inside you do care. That part of you doesn't disappear. It just goes quiet and takes notes. Over time, those notes stack up as low-grade resentment. You might notice:

You feel vaguely "robbed," even if no one has technically stolen anything.

You feel oddly irritated with people you also love—your partner, your boss, your pastor, your parents.

You have occasional disproportionate reactions: snapping over small requests, crying in your car, fantasizing about disappearing.

Your internal monologue sounds like:

"They never consider me."

"They just assume I'll adjust."

"No one ever asks what I want."

Sometimes that's accurate. Sometimes, if we're brutally honest, we never gave them a real "no" to work with.

We trained them.

We taught our boss, "You can keep adding things to my plate; I'll figure it out."

We taught our family, "I'll drive across three states every holiday; it's fine."

We taught our partner, "I don't have strong opinions about money, parenting, where we live—you decide."

And then we quietly seethed. Resentment is what grows in the gap between what you say and what you actually want. The solution is not to become self-centered. The solution is to become congruent.

"I Don't Know What I Want" (And What It Often Really Means).

There's a sentence that sounds humble and harmless:

"I don't know what I want." Sometimes, that's honest. You're truly in a season of figuring it out. But often, if you peel it back a layer, "I don't know" is doing a lot of emotional work. It can mean:

"I've never had the safety to ask that question without getting punished."

"I'm afraid that if I say what I want, I'll lose love, approval, or security."

"I suspect what I want would require a lot of change, and I don't know if I have the energy for that."

"If I admit what I want, I'll have to face how far my current life is from it."

So "I don't know" becomes this soft, padded room where you don't have to deal with: Hope. (What if I want something and don't get it?), Disappointment. (What if I ask and they say no?), Responsibility. (What if I choose and it doesn't work out?). The problem is, "I don't know" also protects you from: Fulfillment. Joy. Alignment.

What if "I don't know what I want" slowly became:

"I'm learning to admit what I want, even when it scares me."

Notice the shift. You don't have to go from blank confusion to full clarity overnight. You just have to be willing to stop using "I don't know" as a shield against your own desire.

Let me tell you the story of: *The Engineer Who "Fell Into" Everything*

Meet Jason. If you read Jason's résumé, you'd think, "Strategic. Intentional. Climbing." Top engineering school. Solid internships. Job at a respected firm. Gradual promotions. Marriage. Two kids. Suburban house. Respectable car. Ask Jason how any of those things happened, and his story sounded different:

"Well, my high-school counselor said engineering was a good stable path."

"My dad really pushed for that university."

"My first boss recommended I go into management track."

"My wife wanted to live near her family, so we bought here."

"My pastor suggested I lead the men's group."

Each choice made sense. None of them felt like a crisis. But sitting in traffic one day, late for a meeting he didn't care about, Jason had a thought that scared him with its clarity:

"I don't remember the last time I made a big decision because I wanted it, not because it was the logical next step or what someone else expected."

He wasn't miserable. He was absent. He had outsourced so much of his decision-making that he no longer trusted his own preferences. When his therapist asked him, "What do you want?" he stared at the ceiling for a long time and finally said, "Honestly? I'm not sure I've ever seriously asked myself that unless it was about what to eat for dinner." That was not a sign of stupidity or weakness.

It was the predictable outcome of a life optimized for being "a good son, a good employee, a good husband, a good church member"—in that order. The work ahead of him wasn't to blow up his life.

It was to start participating in it.

Organizational Currents and the Passive Passenger. Organizations have strong currents. They have strategic plans, cultural norms, "how we do things here." They have implicit tracks: high-potential talent pipelines, "good soldier" lanes, "reliable backbone" roles. If you're not paying attention, you can get swept along by those currents for years. You start in a role "just to get your foot in the door." You're good at it, so you get rewarded with more of the same. You keep saying yes to whatever's in front of you. One day you look up and realize you've become the de facto expert in a niche you never chose. Entire careers are built this way. Sometimes that works out beautifully. You stumble into a lane that genuinely fits you. Other times you end up as, say, the global lead for a process you never cared about, wondering, "How did this become my thing?" In a corporate setting, letting other people move your cheese can sound like: "We think you'd be perfect for this role.", "We really need you on this project.", "You're the only one we trust with this client." Those are flattering sentences. They're also potential traps if you treat them as commands instead of invitations. Because "We need you" is not the same as "This is good for you."

The Difference Between Surrender and Abdication. Sometimes people spiritualize their passivity. "If the door opens, it must be God.", "I'm just trusting the process.", "I'm surrendered." There's a healthy version of that: staying open, not overcontrolling, acknowledging that you can't orchestrate everything. And then there's abdication: quietly exiting the decision-making room of your own life and calling it faith, or fate, or "being laid-back."

- Surrender says, "I bring my real desires, and I hold them loosely."

- Abdication says, "I don't have desires; whatever happens, happens."

Surrender requires a self to show up. Abdication erases the self so there's nothing to surrender. Even if you're not a religious person, the distinction matters. You can collaborate with forces outside your control—market shifts, family realities, organizational decisions—without disappearing. You still get to say, "Given what's happening, here's what I choose."

The Small Places You Hand Over the Pen. We tend to think of agency in terms of big moves: jobs, marriages, relocations. But most of us hand over our cheese in smaller, quieter ways long before those moments. You let your boss tack on "just one more thing" to your workload because you don't want to be "that person" who says it's too much. You let your extended family set every holiday agenda, even though you're exhausted and dreading the travel, because "they'd be so disappointed if we didn't come." You let your partner handle all the financial decisions, not because you truly trust them more, but because money stresses you out and it's easier to say, "Whatever you think is best." You let your church, your culture, or your peer group set the timeline for your milestones—marriage, kids, house, career moves—without ever seriously sitting down to ask, "What do I want this next five years to look like?" Each of these is "no big deal" in the moment. Collectively, they form a pattern.

You're not driving. You're not even in the front seat. You're in the back, hoping the people with their hands on the wheel happen to be heading somewhere you'll like.

Let me tell you the story about: The "Supportive" Spouse Who Vanished

Consider Laura. Laura prided herself on being a supportive spouse. Her husband, Mark, was the classic "big vision" type—always with a new business idea, a new ministry concept, a new move in mind. When they were dating, it was exciting. "We're going places," she thought.

After they married, "we" quietly became "he has ideas; I reorganize my life." When he wanted to move states for a job opportunity, she said, "If that's what you feel led to do, I'm with you." She left a job she liked but told herself, "I can find something similar there."

When he wanted to start a church plant, she said, "If that's your calling, I'll support however I can." Suddenly, her weekends, evenings, and friendships revolved around a community she hadn't actively chosen.

When he wanted to bring his parents to live with them, she said, "Family is important; we'll make it work," even though she knew her bandwidth was already stretched.

If you'd asked her, she would have said, "We make decisions together." Technically, there were conversations. But each time, she defaulted to his preference without ever fully articulating hers.

Ten years in, sitting in a service she hadn't chosen, in a city she hadn't picked, with in-laws she hadn't invited, she had a quiet panic. "I don't know if I want any of this… and I don't know how to say that without feeling like the villain in my own marriage."

The problem wasn't that Mark was evil or controlling. He was used to dreaming out loud and having people organize around him. Laura was used to organizing. They had unconsciously built a life where one person's cheese did most of the moving—and the other person did most of the carrying. The work ahead for Laura wasn't to become the dictator of the relationship. It was to show up as an actual co-author.

When Other People Really Did Move Your Cheese. So far, we've been talking about the subtle ways we allow others to steer. There's another category we need to name: situations where your cheese was moved with very little real consent. Maybe you grew up in poverty, war, or instability, where survival took precedence over preference. You took whatever job kept the lights on. You went where the adults went. You said yes to the opportunities you were given because there weren't others. Maybe you were in a controlling or abusive relationship—romantic, family, spiritual, professional—where your "no" was not just ignored, but punished. In those contexts, passivity wasn't a quirk; it was a safety strategy. Maybe you've faced systemic barriers—racism, sexism, classism, ableism—that limited your choices in ways that had nothing to do with your courage. If that's your story, this chapter is not an invitation to blame yourself for what was done to you. It's an invitation to ask, very gently:

> *"Given what they did, what is one small way I can begin to reclaim some say in what happens next?"*

Maybe that's finding a therapist or coach to help you untangle what's "them" and what's "me."

Maybe it's picking one area of your life—schedule, friendships, hobbies—and making a decision there purely because it matters to you.

Maybe it's letting yourself want something you were always told "people like us don't get."

Agency doesn't always start with the big stuff. Sometimes it starts with choosing how you spend one hour on a Saturday and not apologizing for it.

The Organizational Guilt Trip. In many workplaces, there's a subtle guilt economy around agency. When you start asserting a preference—about workload, career path, boundaries—you may hear:

"You're not being a team player."

"We really need you to step up."

"Everyone else is making sacrifices."

"We thought you were more committed than this."

These phrases are often deployed when your "no" disrupts someone else's convenience. If you've spent years being the reliable yes, the first time you push back will feel like you're betraying the entire company. *You are not. You are disrupting a pattern.*

From the organization's perspective, they've had the luxury of your under-priced labor and over-flexibility for a long time. Any move toward equilibrium feels like loss. From your perspective, you're simply saying, "My life is not an unlimited resource for your plans." Healthy organizations, given time, adjust to that. They may not love it, but they adapt. Unhealthy ones double down on guilt. Recognizing which one you're in is part of moving your cheese on purpose instead of being quietly relocated.

The Awkwardness of Your First Real "No". If you've lived most of your life on default "yes," your first serious "no" will feel like a crime. You'll overexplain. You'll apologize three times. You'll rehearse your sentence in your head like you're preparing for trial. "Thank you for thinking of me, but I can't take that on right now." "I appreciate the offer. It's not the right fit for me." "I need some time to think about this before I commit." You'll hit send or say the words and then immediately want to offer a follow-up email softening it.

Expect some turbulence. People who are used to your automatic yes may react:

"What's going on with you lately?"

"You've changed."

"You're being difficult."

They are not wrong about one thing: you have changed. You've started showing up as an actual person. You don't need to swing to the other extreme and become inflexible or combative. You can stay kind and clear.

Over time, your nervous system will learn that saying no does not, in fact, cause the world to end. Some people will adjust. A few might fall away. You'll survive both.

Let me tell you the story about: The Employee Who Finally Chose Her Own Role

Sofia worked in HR at a mid-size company. For years, she was the unofficial "catch-all." If any department had a problem, they brought it to her. She was good at it. Great, even. The CEO loved to say, "Sofia just gets it done." When a new initiative launched, she was "asked" to lead the culture committee. When a manager flamed out, she was "asked" to step in "temporarily."

When the company decided to host a big conference, she was "asked" to coordinate. Asked, in this case, meant, "We all just assumed you would. You're the only one who can." One performance review cycle, her boss said, "We're so impressed with how you've stepped up across the board. We're thinking of formally moving you into a role where you oversee all of these functions."

It sounded like a promotion. It felt like a sentence. Sofia went home, journaled, and for the first time wrote, *"What do I want my work to be about?"* The answer surprised her: she wanted to go deeper into one area—learning and development—instead of being the company's general-purpose fixer.

The next day, hands shaking, she said to her manager: *"I'm honored you trust me with so much. I've realized that the way I've been working isn't sustainable for me. The role you're proposing doesn't fit what I want to build long-term. I'd like to talk about shaping a position that focuses on L&D instead."*

There was silence.

Then confusion.

Then negotiation.

In the end, she didn't get everything she asked for immediately. But she got something far more important: she put a stake in the ground that said, "I am not just a container for everyone else's needs. I have a direction." That was the day she stopped letting the organization move her cheese by default.

She hadn't left the company. She had finally arrived.

From Passenger to Co-Driver. One of the myths about agency is that you have to be the sole architect of your life or you're failing. That's not how humans work. Our stories are co-written—by family, culture, economics, health, timing, luck, faith, and yes, other people's decisions. You are not in control of everything. But there is a difference between acknowledging that and handing over the keys entirely. You don't have to be the only driver. You do have to be in the front seat. You are allowed to say:

"I hear what you're suggesting. Here's how that lands for me."

"I know this makes sense on paper. It doesn't fit me anymore."

"I'm grateful for your input, and I'm going to choose differently."

"I went along with that before. I won't this time."

You won't always get your way. That's not the point. The point is that you stop living as if your preferences, limits, and longings are an inconvenience everyone else should be spared.

The Intellectually Honest Question. If you want to make this chapter practical, there's one deceptively simple question you can start asking yourself before any medium-to-large decision:

"Do I actually want this, or am I mostly afraid of what will happen if I say no?"

Sit with that. If the honest answer is, "I want it," great. Own that. *Move toward it.* If the honest answer is, "I don't really want it, but I'm scared they'll be disappointed / angry / hurt / inconvenienced," notice that too. You may still choose to say yes. But now you're saying yes consciously, not by reflex. And sometimes, you'll decide that your fear of their reaction is not a good enough reason to keep abandoning yourself. That moment—internal, invisible, barely dramatic—is you, quietly, finally, moving your own cheese.

Not away from everyone.

Just back into your own hands.

CHEESE CHECK

This chapter is about noticing where you've been more passenger than driver in your own life—and gently moving toward the front seat.

Take this slowly.

Where in your life right now do you feel most like things are "just happening" to you?

Work? Family? Church? A relationship? Finances?

Write: "In _____________, I often feel like a passenger, not a driver."

Think of one major past decision that you mostly "went along" with. What was it—school choice, job, move, marriage, ministry, role?

How much of that decision reflected your true desire?

What were you afraid would happen if you had spoken up?

Rejection? Conflict? Disappointment? Being seen as selfish, ungrateful, difficult?

Write the fear in one clear sentence.

Where do you notice quiet resentment in your life? Toward whom? About what?

Complete this sentence:

"I feel resentful when _____________ because I never really said _____________."

Try finishing this sentence without overthinking:

"If I weren't afraid of letting people down, one change I'd seriously consider making is _____________."

Practice one small, honest "no" or "I need time" this week. It could be about a favor, an extra responsibility, a social event, a family expectation.

Plan the sentence now:

"Thank you for asking. I need to think about it and get back to you," or

"I appreciate you asking me, but I can't take that on right now."

Write a blessing over your own agency. Something like: "I am allowed to have preferences. I am allowed to take up space. I am allowed to participate in decisions about my life." You don't have to swing from "I never decide anything" to "It's my way or nothing."

You can start by doing this one radical thing: Showing up as a real person in your own story. In the next chapter, we'll start weaving all of this together and talk about what it means to move your cheese on purpose—with a clear, honest "why," instead of just reacting to life or repeating old patterns.

CHEESE CHECK NOTES

Your heart may be afraid and still say,

"This is right."

Your heart may be relieved and still say,

"Something in this isn't honest."

Listen.

Dr. Laide R. Alexander

CHAPTER SEVEN

Moving Your Cheese On Purpose

By now, you've seen a lot of ways cheese can move:

- Life moves it, and you're left standing in shock.
- You move it to survive.
- You move it to grow.
- You move it to hide.
- You don't move it at all—you let other people move it for you.

If you're thinking, "I see myself in all of these," that's not a problem. That means you're human. The goal of this book is not to put every move you've ever made into a "good" or "bad" category. The goal is this: To help you move your cheese on purpose — with a clear, honest why — instead of just reacting, repeating old patterns, or disappearing. This chapter is about what it looks like to make intentional moves. Not perfect moves. Not guaranteed-to-work-out moves. Intentional ones.

The Difference Between Reacting and Choosing. Let's start with a simple distinction. Reacting sounds like: "They did this, so I had to…" "I was just over it, so I left." "I panicked and made a decision." "I didn't think it through; I just needed out."

Choosing sounds like:

- "I took time to understand what was happening in me."

- "I named my options and the likely consequences."
- "I aligned my decision with my values, not just my feelings."
- "I didn't know everything, but I knew enough to move with integrity."

Reacting is usually fast, emotional, and about relief. Choosing is often slower, uncomfortable, and about alignment. Relief says, "Make this feeling stop." Alignment says, "Make this decision true to who I am becoming." Sometimes, you will have to move fast. Life doesn't always give you weeks to journal. But even then, you can pause long enough to ask one powerful question: "Am I running from something… or moving toward something?" The more often you can answer that honestly, the more intentional your moves become.

Your "Why" Is Your Steering Wheel. Think of your "why" as the steering wheel of your move. Same action, different why, completely different impact: You leave a job. To survive? To grow? To hide? To please someone else? You step away from a ministry. Because you're burned out? Called elsewhere? Avoiding accountability? You end a relationship. For safety? For growth? For fear of intimacy? Because others disapprove? You move to a new city. To chase a dream? To reset your life? To outrun your grief? If you don't know your why, your move will drive you. If you do know your "why," you can drive your move—even when the road gets bumpy. A clear why doesn't remove all doubt. It just gives you an anchor when doubt shows up.

Four Questions Before You Move Your Cheese. Before you make a major move, here are four questions worth sitting with. They're simple, not easy.

What pain am I trying to stop? Be brutally honest. Is it emotional, physical, spiritual, financial, relational? Am I trying to stop all discomfort, or something that's genuinely harmful?

What possibility am I trying to create? What do I hope will be more true after this move—about my life, my health, my calling, my relationships? **What part of this situation is actually about me? What patterns, fears, or habits am I bringing into this?** If I don't address them, will they follow me into the next place? **What will this cost me—and am I willing to pay it?** Every move costs something: money, time, comfort, status, relationships, certainty. Pretending the cost isn't real doesn't make it go away. Seeing the cost clearly helps you own the move like an adult, not a runaway. If you can't answer these questions yet, it doesn't mean you shouldn't move. It means you shouldn't move mindlessly.

The Myth of the "No-Cost" Move. One reason we get stuck is we secretly wait for the perfect move: All gain, no loss. All confirmation, no doubt. Everyone claps, no one is disappointed. More money, less work. More freedom, no responsibility. Deeper love, zero vulnerability. That move doesn't exist. Every real move has a trade-off:

- You leave the toxic job and lose the predictable paycheck.

- You leave the familiar church and lose the built-in community.

- You stop being the fixer in your family and lose the feeling of being "needed."

- You start the business and lose the illusion of guaranteed security.

- You choose authenticity and lose some approval.

If you wait for a move that costs nothing, you will wait forever. Maturity sounds like: I know what this will cost me. I know what staying will cost me too. I am choosing which cost I'm willing to live with."

The Three Checks: Head, Heart, and History. Before you move your cheese, it can help to check in with three parts of you.

1. **HEAD —The Logic Check**

   Ask:

   - What are the facts, not just my feelings?

   - What are my real options? (Not just the dramatic ones.)

   - What resources do I have? (Skills, money, support, time.)

   - What's my plan for the first 3–6 months after this move?

You don't need a 50-page business plan - leave a situation that's killing you. But you also don't want to leap without any thought and call it faith when it's really panic.

2. HEART —The Integrity Check

Ask:

- Does this move align with my deepest values?

- Am I becoming more of who I say I want to be… or less?

- When I imagine explaining this decision to a future, wiser version of myself, how does it feel?

Your heart may be afraid and still say, "This is right." Your heart may be relieved and still say, "Something in this isn't honest." *Listen.*

3. HISTORY —The Pattern Check

Ask:

- How does this decision fit my past patterns?

- Does it look like my old survival moves, growth moves, hiding moves, or passive non-moves?

- Am I repeating an old story with new characters?

History doesn't get to dictate your future. But it would be wise to let it inform your choices.

Making Room for Both Faith and Wisdom. If you're a person of faith, you may feel pulled between: *"Just trust God and jump!"* and *"Be wise, plan everything,* don't you dare make a mistake.*"* Here's the truth: *You can do both.* Faith without any wisdom can turn into recklessness. Wisdom without any faith can turn into fear dressed up as "prudence." A more balanced posture might sound like: *"I'm praying and paying attention." "I'm taking counsel,* and, *I'm listening for God's nudge in my own spirit." "I'm willing to move without absolute certainty, but not without any clarity."* Sometimes you won't get confirmation until you move. Sometimes you'll get a clear "no" or "not yet," and part of moving on purpose is respecting that. Faith is not the absence of questions. Faith is the decision to move in the direction of what you know, even while you're still holding what you don't know.

How to Talk About Your Move Without Lying. One subtle way we lose ourselves is by telling dishonest stories about our decisions:

- We make ourselves the complete hero—or the complete victim.

- We erase the parts that were about fear, ego, or avoidance.

- We exaggerate how bad "they" were so we never have to look at our part.

If you want to move your cheese on purpose, practice honest storytelling. Instead of:

"They were all toxic, so I left." Try: "There were unhealthy dynamics I couldn't change. And there were parts of me I didn't know how to bring honestly, so I chose to leave."

Instead of: "God told me to leave, end of story." Try: "I sensed God leading me in a different direction. I was also tired and hurt, and that played a role. I'm learning from all of it."

Instead of: *"I had no choice."* Try: *"I didn't like my options. I chose the one that felt most aligned, even though it was hard."* You don't owe everyone your whole truth. But you owe yourself a story that doesn't require you to lie, demonize, or disappear.

Leaving Room for Regret—Without Letting It Rule You. Even intentional moves can lead to moments of regret. You may find yourself thinking: "Did I make a mistake?", "Maybe I should've stayed.", "Maybe I moved too fast.", "What if I never find something this good again?" Regret is not proof you made the wrong decision. It's proof you're human enough to feel the weight of your choices. When regret shows up, you can: ***Listen to it***. Is it showing you a real blind spot?

Is there something you need to apologize for, learn from, or do differently next time? ***Limit it.***

Don't let it become your narrator. "I might have done some things differently" is not the same as "I ruin everything." ***Let it grow you.*** Regret can become wisdom instead of a life sentence. You can say, "I see more now than I did then. I bless the me who made that choice with what they knew." Moving on purpose doesn't mean you'll never look back. It means you don't let looking back paralyze you.

Giving Yourself Permission to Stay. One more important piece; Sometimes, after all this reflection, you'll realize: "For now… I'm not going to move my cheese." That can be just as intentional as leaving. You might decide to:

- Stay in the job but renegotiate your role or boundaries

- Stay in the relationship but insist on counseling or new patterns

- Stay in the church but move into a different way of serving

- Stay in the city but change how you live within it

- Staying on purpose is different from staying by default.

Default staying says: "It's too hard to think about changing anything." "This is just my life, I guess." **Intentional staying** says: "I've looked at my options. I'm choosing to stay for now, and here's what I'm going to do differently while I'm here." Sometimes the most powerful move you can make is to stay—awake, honest, and engaged. By this point in the book, you've seen cheese flying everywhere.

Sometimes life yanks it out of your hands.

Sometimes you drag it across the floor to stay alive.

Sometimes you move it toward something bigger.

Sometimes you carry it into a new maze just to hide.

Sometimes you stand there politely while other people rearrange it for you.

If you're thinking, "Unfortunately, I have done all of these," that doesn't mean you're broken.

It means you're awake. This chapter is not about grading your past moves. It's about what comes now: learning to move your cheese on purpose—with a clear, honest, grown-up "why"—instead of just reacting, repeating, or disappearing. Not perfect moves. Not guaranteed-to-work moves. Intentional ones.

1. Reaction vs. Choice: Same Move, Different Story. At first glance, reacting and choosing can look the same from the outside. Two people leave the same job. One says, "I was done. They disrespected me, so I bounced." , The other says, "I paid attention to how this place was changing and how I was changing. I made a call."

Same outcome: resignation letter.

Different posture: one was flung out of a slingshot; the other walked out of a door.

Reaction is usually about relief.

"Make this feeling stop.

Make this person go away.

Make this situation disappear."

Choice is usually about alignment." Make this decision match who I am and who I want to become." Reaction is fast, hot, and narrow. Your field of vision shrinks to the thing that hurts. Choice is slower, uncomfortable, and wider. You still see the pain, but you also see the pattern, the context, the cost of staying and the cost of leaving. You won't always have weeks to sit on a mountain with a journal. Sometimes the building really is on fire. Sometimes the layoff is tomorrow. Sometimes the relationship is crossing lines you cannot un-cross. Even then, you can usually pause long enough to ask one small but sharp question:

"Am I mostly running from something or moving toward something?"

You can still move either way. But the more often you answer that question honestly, the more your life stops feeling like a string of explosions and starts feeling like a series of decisions.

2. Your "Why" Is the Steering Wheel. Imagine two people making the same move: both moving to a new city. Person A is leaving because every corner of the old city reminds them of a breakup they refuse to grieve. Person B is leaving because the industry they want to be in is centered there, and they're ready to bet on themselves.

Same action: new lease, new DMV nightmare, new coffee shop. Different *"why."*

The **"why"** is what you grab when the honeymoon ends. Because it will end. The new job will have annoying people. The new church will have weird traditions. The new city will have days that smell like trash. The new relationship will have conflict. On those days, if your move was powered by "I just needed to get away," you'll be tempted to keep running. If it was powered by "This move fits what I'm trying to build," you'll have something sturdier to hold onto than mood swings.

Your why is your steering wheel.

"I left that role because I refused to keep normalizing burnout as leadership."

"I stepped back from that volunteer work because I was doing it for approval, not conviction."

"I ended that relationship because I was becoming someone I didn't respect."

"I stayed in that city because I chose depth over novelty—for this season."

You don't need a TED-Talk-ready answer.

You just need a sentence you can say to yourself without flinching.

3. Four Questions to Ask Before You Move the Cheese. Before you do anything dramatic with your life, it helps to interrogate the move a little. Think of these four questions as the annoying but wise friend who makes you slow down before you hit "send."

3.1 What pain am I trying to stop? Not the Instagram version. The actual one. Is it:

Exhaustion?	Disrespect?
Loneliness?	Boredom?
Shame?	Constant anxiety?
Financial strain?	Feeling invisible?

Are you trying to stop: A specific, harmful pattern? ("My boss belittles me in front of others weekly."), Or all discomfort, period?, ("I never want to feel challenged or exposed again."), Those are different projects. Leaving a job because your health is collapsing is different from leaving because you don't like being new at things. Breaking up with someone who violates your boundaries is different from breaking up the moment they see a side of you that isn't curated. If you can name the real pain, you can reality-check whether your move addresses it—or just relocates it.

Sometimes the move is necessary. Sometimes the move is a painkiller with nasty side effects.

3.2 What possibility am I trying to create? Pain pushes. Possibility pulls. If you only ever move away from things, your life becomes one long game of emotional dodgeball.

What do you want to move toward? Not in vague terms like "more peace" or "more money." Be specific enough that someone else could spot it. "I want work where my contribution is measurable and not constantly crisis-driven.", "I want a relationship where conflict isn't a monthly catastrophe.", "I want to live somewhere I'm not the only person who looks/works/thinks like me.", "I want a schedule that leaves room for my body not to be a machine." Possibility doesn't have to be grand. "I want to be able to sleep through the night without checking my email at 2 a.m." is a perfectly respectable north star.

3.3 What part of this is actually about me? This is the least fun question and the most useful.

You don't have to take all the blame for every bad situation. That's not maturity; that's martyrdom. But there is almost always a slice of the pie that's yours. Did you keep saying yes when you meant no?

Did you ignore red flags because the benefits were good?, Did you enjoy being "indispensable" a little too much?, Did you expect people to read your mind instead of stating your needs?, Did you assume your patterns wouldn't follow you into this place because "this time is different"?

The goal here is not self-flagellation. It's leverage.

Because if your only post-move narrative is, "They were awful; I was flawless," you'll be perfectly set up to re-enact the same dynamic with a different cast.

3.4 What will this cost me—and am I willing to pay it? Every move has a bill.

Leave or stay, you pay something. Leaving might cost you stability, community, status, familiarity, a clear identity. Staying might cost you energy, health, opportunities, self-respect, time. Pretending there's a no-cost option is how people end up in decade-long holding patterns. If you write the costs down—literally, on paper—they become less mystical and more measurable. "I'm willing to give up X to gain a shot at Y." "I'm not willing to sacrifice A, so I need a different plan." You might still be scared.

Fear is not a veto. But when you can say, "I see the price tag, and I'm choosing this anyway," you've shifted from being dragged to walking.

4. The Myth of the Perfect, Painless Move. There's a fantasy move a lot of us secretly wait for:

Zero risk

All upside

Applause from everyone

No one hurt, no one confused

More money, less work

More meaning, no discomfort

New love, no heartbreak potential

This move does not exist on the actual planet.

Every move, even the right one, has a "but":

"I left the toxic job… but I miss the stability."

"I left the small, tight-knit church… but I miss how quickly people showed up when I needed help."

"I stopped being the fixer in my family… but I miss being everyone's hero."

"I started my own business… but now I wake up at 3 a.m. thinking about cash flow."

"I chose authenticity… but some people really did walk away."

If you wait for a move that satisfies everyone, threatens nothing, and costs you nothing, you'll still be in the same chair five years from now, calling it "waiting on clarity." Sometimes what we call "I'm just discerning" is really "I'm shopping for a life change with no trade-offs." Maturity is less glamorous. It sounds like: "I know what this will cost.

I know what staying will cost. I am choosing which regret I'm willing to live with."

5. The Three Checks: Head, Heart, History. Before you move your cheese in any big way, it can help to do three quick internal audits.

5.1 Head: The Logic Check. This is not "overthink until you're paralyzed."

It's "think at least enough that you won't be shocked by predictable consequences."

Useful questions:

- What are the actual facts, not just my feelings?
- (Layoff rumors are facts. "My boss hates me" might be a feeling.)

- What are my real options?
- (Not just "stay forever" vs. "quit tomorrow." There is often a middle path.)
- What resources do I have? (Savings, skills, support, time, mental bandwidth.)
- What's my plan for the first 3–6 months after this move? (Not the rest of my life. Just the next stretch.)

You don't need a 50-page business plan to leave a job that's wrecking your health. But quitting without any plan and calling it "faith" when it's actually panic is how people end up right back in another bad situation—just more desperate. Think enough to respect future you. They're the one who has to live in whatever you build.

5.2 Heart: The Integrity Check, Logic can tell you whether something is plausible. Integrity tells you whether it's true to you. Questions here sound like:

Does this move line up with the kind of person I say I want to be?

Am I doing this mostly out of fear, spite, ego, or avoidance?

If I explained this decision to a version of me 10 years older and wiser, would I feel proud, embarrassed, or somewhere in between?

Sometimes your heart will be terrified and still quietly say, "This is right." Sometimes your heart will feel instant relief and still whisper, "We're not being entirely honest about why we're doing this."

You don't have to obey every feeling. But ignoring them altogether is how you end up with a "successful" move that still feels like a self-betrayal.

5.3 History: The Pattern Check. If you never look back, you will keep walking into the same wall and calling it "God testing me" or "the universe hating me" or "other people always doing me wrong."

Patterns aren't destiny, but they're very solid data. Ask:

How does this move resemble past ones?

Is this starting to look like my classic survival exit? My classic freak-out quit? My classic "upgrade" that's just a shinier version of the same thing?

Am I expecting a new environment to magically fix a pattern I have never actually worked on?

If every job you've left has involved a last-minute blowup and a bridge on fire, it might be worth asking why you wait until you're at combustion point to honor your limits. If every relationship ends right after the other person says, "Hey, can we talk about something that's bothering me?" that's not a coincidence. Patterns don't get to be the judge. But they should absolutely be called as witnesses.

6. Planning Without Worshiping the Plan. Some people never move their cheese because they're still making the spreadsheet.

They want every variable controlled. They research until the opportunity expires. They build contingency plans for contingencies. Underneath, it's not wisdom. It's terror of being wrong.

On the other end, you have the people who treat thoughtfulness like a sin. "Plans are for cowards. Real ones just jump." They fetishize chaos. Every move is a leap. No scaffolding, no runway, just vibes. Underneath, that's often terror of being still long enough to feel anything. Moving on purpose lives in the middle. You think enough to not blindside yourself. You risk enough that there is something at stake. You can:

Run the numbers and admit they're an estimate.

Talk to people who've done what you're considering and know you're not living their life.

Make a six-month plan and hold it loosely, because reality always edits.

The plan is not the point. *The point is that you showed up to your own decision.*

7. Telling the Truth About Your Move (At Least to Yourself). We are master storytellers when it comes to our own decisions.

We're the hero in our favorite versions. Or the helpless victim. Rarely the complex human who did the best they could with mixed motives. When you move your cheese, you will be tempted to craft a simple story:

"They were all toxic."

"I had no choice."

"God told me, end of story."

"It was either this or die."

Sometimes that's… close. But simple stories are rarely whole stories. An honest narrative might sound like:

"There were dynamics at that job I couldn't change, and they were harming me. I also waited too long to set boundaries, and that made it worse. Leaving was the right call. I wish I'd done it earlier and cleaner."

Or:

"I say I left that relationship because we 'grew apart.' The truth is, I was too afraid to bring my full self, and they stopped trusting that I was really there. Ending it was necessary by the time I did it, but I'm learning from how I showed up."

You don't owe this level of nuance to everyone. Your LinkedIn post can be, "Excited for what's next!" Your grandma can get the PG-13 version. But you deserve a story that doesn't require you to erase your own complexity. Because if you lie to yourself about why you moved, you'll have to keep living a life built on that lie.

8. Making Space for Regret Without Letting It Drive. Even the best, most intentional moves will have you lying awake some nights asking:

"What if I stayed?"

"What if I blew it?"

"What if this never works?"

Regret is not a sign you made the wrong choice. It's a sign you are aware that choices have weight. You can do three things with regret:

8.1 Listen to It. Sometimes regret is pointing at something real.

"I wish I hadn't said it like that."

"I see now that I hurt people on my way out."

"I didn't understand how much I'd miss that part."

You can apologize. You can adjust. You can take the note for next time.

8.2 Limit It. Regret loves to audition for the role of narrator. It wants to turn "I could have handled that better" into "I ruin everything I touch."

You can say, "No, you get to be a consultant. Not the CEO."

8.3 Let It Grow You. If you can look back at a past decision and say, "I would do some things differently now," that's not evidence of failure. That's evidence of growth. You know more now. You see more now. You can bless the earlier version of you: "They were doing the best they could with what they knew," and then make this next move with upgraded data. Moving on purpose doesn't mean you never look back over your shoulder.

It means you don't live back there anymore.

9. Permission to Stay—On Purpose. Sometimes, after all this self-interrogation, you'll land on a surprising conclusion:

"For now… I'm not going to move my cheese."

That can be just as intentional—and just as brave—as leaving.

There's a big difference between:

"I'm staying because thinking about change makes me tired,"

and

"I'm staying because, given my options, this is the best place for me to grow right now, and I'm going to treat it that way."

Intentional staying might look like:

Same company, different role—or same role, different boundaries.

Same relationship, new patterns.

Same city, new routines, new community.

Same church, different expectations and involvement.

Default staying sounds like, "This is just my life, I guess."

Conscious staying sounds like, "I'm here on purpose, and while I'm here, I'm going to do X, Y, and Z differently." The move isn't always geographic or professional. Sometimes the move is internal: you don't leave the maze, but you stop running in circles.

10. Micro-Moves: Practicing Purpose in Small Decisions. It's tempting to think intentionality only applies to the big life shifts.

But the way you handle small decisions is rehearsal for how you'll handle the big ones. Micro-moves look like: Saying, *"Let me think about it,"* instead of reflexively saying yes to every request. Choosing one evening a week that is protected from work, church, and family demands—and not apologizing for it. Turning down a "great opportunity" that doesn't fit your actual goals, just to prove to yourself you can. Asking for what you want in low-stakes situations (the restaurant, the movie, the weekend plan) so your nervous system learns that having preferences is not a crime. These seem trivial.

They are not. They are how you teach your brain, "My voice matters in my own life."

Then, when it's time to make a bigger move, you're not trying to lift 200 pounds of agency with muscles you've never used.

11. Moving With Others Without Losing Yourself. Most of us don't move our cheese in isolation. We have partners, kids, parents, teams, congregations. The myth of the solo hero making clean decisions in a vacuum is just that—a myth. Intentional moves in community are messy. You want to leave; your partner wants to stay. You're ready to change careers; your parents are panicking about your résumé. You feel done with a role; your team is begging you to hold on "just a little longer."

Moving on purpose doesn't mean you bulldoze other people. It also doesn't mean you let their fear have more say than your own conscience. *The work is in:*

Being honest earlier instead of springing decisions on people once they're final.

Listening—really listening—to their concerns, not just waiting for your turn to speak.

Separating their preferences from your responsibility. ("I prefer you never change anything" is not a binding contract.)

Being willing to adjust how you move without surrendering whether you move.

Sometimes you'll delay a move to coordinate with a partner's timeline. Sometimes you'll scale it. Sometimes you'll still go, and they'll still be upset.

There's no version where everyone claps and no one hurts.

There is *a version where you can say, "I heard you. I factored you in. I still had to choose this."*

That's adulthood.

12. When the Move Is Internal, Not External. Not every purposeful move involves a resignation, a U-Haul, or a breakup. Sometimes the most radical cheese-shift is internal:

You stop being available 24/7 in the same role and start acting like a human with limits. You decide to stop treating your job as your entire identity and start acting like it's one part of a bigger life. You shift from "I'm lucky to be here" to "I bring real value, and I'm allowed to ask for what I'm worth." You choose to tell the truth in spaces where you've always performed. From the outside, nothing seems different. Same desk. Same address. Same ring on your finger.

On the inside, you have quietly moved your cheese from "out there" (what everyone thinks, what everyone needs) to "in here" (what I know, what I believe, what I will and won't do).

Those internal moves often cause external ones later. But they don't wait for permission.

13. Designing a Life Where Moves Aren't Always Emergencies. If every move you make is happening at the edge of collapse, your nervous system will start to associate change with panic. One of the long-term goals of moving on purpose is to build a life where not every shift is a five-alarm fire. That looks like: Checking in with yourself quarterly, not once every seven years. Adjusting roles, boundaries, and commitments while you still have energy—not when you're already toast. Saying, "This setup worked for me at 28; it doesn't at 38," before you sabotage it out of boredom. Letting smaller, more frequent moves prevent the need for giant, explosive ones. Think of it like steering on a highway.

Tiny course corrections keep you in your lane. If you only touch the wheel when you're about to hit the median, every adjustment feels catastrophic.

14. A Different Way to Measure "Success" of a Move. We're used to evaluating moves by their external outcomes.

Did the new job pay more?

Did the business succeed?

Did the relationship last?

Did the ministry grow?

Those are not irrelevant questions. But if that's all you measure, you'll miss the deeper point. A move can look like a failure on paper and still be a success for your development. If you took a role and realized in six months, "This is not it," but in that time you:

Learned what kind of work environment you never want again,

Practiced negotiating your exit without ghosting,

Discovered you're more resilient than you thought, that move wasn't wasted.

If you left a church or community and, in the messy aftermath, finally confronted patterns in yourself you'd been avoiding for years, that's not just "church hurt." *That's data.*

The deeper question after a move is: "*Who did I become in the process of making and living with this decision?*" If the answer is, "Someone a little more honest, a little more responsible for their own life," then even if the externals were rough, something important succeeded.

15. Moving Your Cheese on Purpose: A Working Definition. Let's pull this together. Moving your cheese on purpose does not mean: You always know exactly what you're doing. Everyone agrees with your choices. The move works out exactly how you planned.

You never feel fear, regret, or confusion.

It means something quieter and more demanding: You stop outsourcing your major life decisions to crisis, convenience, or other people's comfort.

You take the time you can take to understand your pain, your patterns, and your possibilities.

You tell yourself the truth about your motives, even when you don't tell everyone else.

You accept the cost of your choices without making yourself the hero or the victim in every story.

You allow both your head and your heart and your history to speak into the decision—none of them running the show alone.

You're willing to stay when staying is aligned, and willing to leave when leaving is aligned, and willing to be misunderstood either way.

That's it. Not glamorous. Not meme-able. But if you start living like that, slowly, your life will shift from "Things just keep happening to me" to "I'm actively participating in what happens next." ***The cheese will still move.*** Life will still surprise you. But now, when it's time to move it yourself, you won't just grab it and run. You'll pick it up, look at where you've been, look at where you're going, and, with as much clarity as you have that day, say:

"This time, I know why I'm putting it here."

CHEESE CHECK

This chapter is about shifting from automatic to intentional.

Use these questions to practice moving your cheese on purpose.

Think of a move you are currently considering. Job, relationship, ministry, city, role, boundary, schedule? Write it as clearly as you can:

"I am considering ___________."

What pain are you trying to stop with this move? Be specific (burnout, disrespect, boredom, fear, loneliness, financial strain). On a scale of 1–10, how urgent is that pain?

What possibilities are you hoping to create? More peace? Growth? Time? Money? Health? Alignment with your calling? Finish the sentence:

"If this move goes reasonably well, my life will look more like ___________."

How does this move fit your past patterns? Does it look more like survival, growth, hiding, or letting others decide? What does that pattern tell you to be careful about this time?

What will this move cost you—and what will staying cost you? List at least 3 costs of moving and 3 costs of staying. Which cost are you more willing to live with a year from now?

What would it look like to make this move with integrity? Is there a conversation you need to have?
An apology to offer? A plan to put in place? Support you need to gather before or as you move?

If you decided not to move right now, what would intentional staying look like? What one boundary, habit, or conversation would you commit to in order to honor yourself where you are?

Write this final sentence, even if you're not sure of the details yet:

"Whatever I choose next, I refuse to sleepwalk through it. I will move—or stay—on purpose, with a clear and honest why."

In the next chapter, we'll start looking at how to rebuild and re-center your life after a move—how to live with your new cheese without constantly reaching back for the old, and how to walk in your decisions with more peace and less second-guessing.

CHEESE CHECK NOTES

Living with new cheese is hard

when the old voices are still loud in your head.

Dr. Laide R. Alexander

CHAPTER EIGHT

Living With Your New Cheese

Making a move is one thing. Learning to live with the move is another.

You can: Survive the breakup… and still check their page every week. Leave the job… and still measure your worth by that old title. Step away from the church… and still hear those voices in your head. Start the business… and still think like an employee. Set the boundary… and still feel guilty every time you honor it. In other words: You can move your cheese and still mentally live in the old maze. This chapter is about what happens after the move—how to settle into your new reality without constantly dragging the old one behind you like carry-on luggage.

The "Did I Really Do That?" Phase. Right after a big move, there's often a strange quiet. You wake up one day and think:

- "Wait… I really left."
- "I really said that."
- "I really signed those papers."
- "I really started this thing."

It can feel: Surreal. Exhilarating. Terrifying. All of the above before breakfast. This is normal. Your body might already know you needed this. Your spirit might even feel lighter. But your mind is still catching up. You may find yourself: Replaying the last day at the old job, rehearsing old arguments in the shower, imagining how people are talking about you, fantasizing about going back "just to check in. Your brain is not trying to sabotage you. It's trying to make sense of a new map. *Give it time.*

Withdrawal From the Old You

Any time you leave a familiar life, you go through a form of withdrawal. You're not just detoxing from: The job. The relationship. The church. The city. You're detoxing from the you, you were in that place. You may miss being "needed" all the time, having a full calendar, knowing exactly what to do, being the go-to person and the adrenaline of always being in crisis. You might even miss; the drama, the chaos, and the struggle story you knew how to tell. It's uncomfortable to admit, but sometimes we are addicted to our own exhaustion and importance. You might notice you feel strangely guilty when you rest, you're tempted to fill your new space with old-pattern busyness, or you start hunting for a new crisis to prove you're still "useful." ***That's withdrawal.*** It doesn't mean you made the wrong move. It means your nervous system is used to living on fumes.

The Echoes of Old Voices. Living with new cheese is hard when the old voices are still loud in your head:

- "Who do you think you are?"
- "You had a good thing and walked away."
- "You're not going to make it out there."
- "God didn't tell you to do all that."
- "You're selfish."
- "You're ungrateful."
- "You'll be back."

Sometimes those voices came from real people. Sometimes they came from:
- Childhood
- Culture.

- Church teaching.

- Past trauma.

- Your own inner critic.

You can't always stop the echo. But you can decide what you do when it shows up. A simple practice:

Name the voice. *"That's my old pastor talking." "That's my mom's fear." "That's 16-year-old me who felt like a burden."* Name your reality. "I am an adult making the best decision I can with what I know now." "I am allowed to learn in public." "I don't have to stay small to be loved." Over time, the echoes get quieter—not because they never speak, but because you stop treating them as the only truth.

Don't Rush to Prove It Was Worth It. A sneaky pressure shows up after a big move: "Now I have to prove this was the right decision." So you: Overwork in the new job or business to show you're "killing it." Rush into a new relationship to prove you're "over it." Overshare your "healing" online so no one sees your doubt. Make every update a testimony of unbothered success. Underneath that is fear:

- "If this doesn't look amazing fast, people will think I messed up."

- "If I struggle here, I'll have to admit I didn't know everything."

- "If I'm not instantly happy, maybe they were right about me."

Here's the truth: Every real move has an awkward middle. You left the old place. You haven't fully grown into the new one. You are not failing. You're in transit. You don't owe anyone a highlight reel while you're still unpacking boxes.

Building New Rhythms for a New Life. New cheese needs new rhythms. You cannot live your new life with all the habits of your old one and expect to feel different. Ask yourself: What did my old life run on? Constant urgency?

People-pleasing? Overcommitting? Hiding? Passive "going along"? What do I want this new life to run on?

- Clarity?

- Rest?

- Boundaries?

- Creativity?

- Honesty?

- A sustainable pace?

Then—this is important—pick small, boring practices that match your new values. For example: If you left a toxic job for health: Commit to one non-negotiable health practice (a walk, bedtime, a therapy appointment). If you left a draining ministry role for wholeness: Commit to attending somewhere you can receive without performing for a season. If you left a relationship to find yourself again: Commit to one weekly activity that's just for you—no approval, no audience.

Big moves are sustained by small daily choices.

Making Peace With People's Opinions (and Silence). After you move, people will respond in different ways: Some will cheer. Some will question. Some will gossip. Some will quietly disappear. Some will act like nothing happened. Some will wait to see if you "fail" or "come back." You may never get: *The apology. The understanding. The closure.* The *"You did the right thing"* you imagined. Learning to live with your new cheese means accepting a hard but freeing reality: You can't build your new life on other people's reactions to your decision. Their opinion may sting. Their confusion may hurt. But your job is not to convert everyone to your side of the story. Your job is to live this chapter with as much integrity, honesty, and courage as you can. Time has a way of telling the truth. *So does your fruit.*

When the New Place Isn't Perfect Either. At some point, your new situation will show its flaws. The new job has politics, too. The new church has imperfect people. The new city gets lonely. The new relationship reveals both of your patterns. The new "dream" role still has emails and spreadsheets. When this happens, you'll be tempted to say: *"See? I shouldn't have left." "Nothing is ever different." "I traded one mess for another."* Sometimes that's partially true. But often, what's really happening is: You've entered the real part of the story. The goal was never to find a place with no problems. The goal was to find a place where: The problems don't require you to abandon yourself, the stretching leads to growth, not destruction, you can show up as a whole person, not a costume. Instead of asking, "Is this perfect?" try: *"Is this healthier?" "Am I more myself here?" "Are these problems I'm willing to work with?"* **Perfection was never the point. Freedom and alignment were.**

Letting Yourself Be New Here. One of the kindest things you can do for yourself after a move is to let yourself be new. New to: The role. The environment. The boundaries. The version of you that made this choice. Give yourself permission to say: "I've never done this before." "I'm learning how I want to show up in this season." "I don't have to be who I was over there." "I can adjust this as I go." You are not obligated to: Carry old expectations. Keep old personas. Maintain old levels of over functioning. You can discover:

- New ways you like to work.
- New ways you like to rest.
- New ways you like to connect.
- New ways you like to be with God, yourself, and others.

Moving your cheese was the door. Becoming new in how you live with it is the walk through the house.

When You're Tempted to Go Back. There will be days when the old life looks better in the rearview mirror than it ever was in real time. You'll remember: Only the good parts. Only the familiar comforts. Only the highlight moments. You'll forget: The tears in the parking lot. The way your body used to tighten on Sunday nights. The version of you that was disappearing. In those moments, ask yourself: *What am I really missing?* The actual place… or the feeling of certainty, familiarity, or being needed? What need did that old situation meet that I haven't built into my new life yet? Community? Structure? A sense of purpose? Routine? Is going back truly an act of health—or nostalgia and fear? If you went back, what would need to be radically different for it to be safe and right for you? Sometimes people do go back—to a job, a city, even a relationship—but as a different person, with different terms, and a different level of honesty. Other times, going back is simply going backwards. Only you (with wise counsel) can discern the difference.

Blessing Your Old Cheese, Embracing Your New. Here's a practice that can help you live in the present without erasing your past: *Bless your old cheese. Embrace your new.* You can say: "That place/season/role fed me for a while. It taught me things. It gave me people, experiences, and skills I still carry. It also had limits and harms I can no longer ignore. I release it with gratitude and grief. And I choose to be fully present with the life I have now." You don't have to hate where you came from to love where you're going. You can hold both: *"That was real." "This is real, too."*

You can honor the old chapter without reopening the book every night. You can make a life-changing decision in an afternoon. You click "send" on the resignation email. You sign the lease in a new city. You end the relationship. You tell the team, "I'm stepping down." The moment itself is sharp, defined, almost cinematic. You could circle it on a calendar. But living with that decision is not cinematic. It's not one dramatic scene. It's dozens of quiet, ordinary days where you're trying to figure out how to inhabit the life you just chose. *You moved your cheese. Now what?*

This chapter is about that "now what." Not the rush of courage it took to move. The slower, more complex work of learning how to live with your new cheese without constantly dragging your old maze around behind you like an emotional carry-on.

The Hangover After the Big Decision. There's usually a moment—often a surprisingly normal morning—when the reality of what you've done hits you. You wake up and realize you don't have to log into the old systems anymore. Your badge doesn't work at that building. Your name is off the schedule. Your key doesn't fit that door. There is no "we" to text goodnight. You think, with a mix of disbelief and a little adrenaline: "Wait. I really left." Or, "I actually started this. It's not theoretical anymore."

The paperwork is done. The moving truck has come and gone. The conversations have been had. Outwardly, the move is complete. Internally, you feel like someone who shaved their head and keeps reaching up to adjust hair that's no longer there. Your reflexes are still calibrated to an old reality. You might catch yourself opening the work email you no longer have.

You might instinctively drive toward the old office out of habit. You might still mentally rehearse what you're going to say to a person you no longer have regular access to. If you've been in a role, relationship, or community for a long time, your sense of self and your sense of place are entangled. You changed the place. Your sense of self is still unspooling. That disorientation doesn't mean you were wrong to move. It means your mind is catching up to your life.

Detoxing From Your Old Identity. Leaving a situation is one kind of loss. Leaving an identity is another. When you stepped out of the job, you didn't just lose tasks and colleagues. You lost being "the one everyone came to" or "the person who could fix anything" or "the steady one who always stayed late." When you stepped out of the relationship, you didn't just lose a partner. You lost being "the responsible one" or "the forgiving one" or "the one who kept it together." Those roles may have been exhausting, but they were familiar. They gave you a script. They gave you a way to feel significant.

Now you're in a new space with fewer clear lines. No one automatically turns to you first. Fewer fires are your responsibility. Your calendar isn't crowded with other people's emergencies. You have hours in the day that are not already spoken for.

At first, this feels like freedom. Then, weirdly, it feels like loss. You may find yourself missing things you never thought you would: the constant messages, the frantic pace, the high-stakes decisions, the sense that if you didn't show up, everything would fall apart. It's uncomfortable to admit you miss your own burnout, but it's honest. Burnout, over time, can become a kind of identity drug. You hate it, but you also don't quite know who you are without the rush. So you feel the itch to recreate it. You're tempted to fill your new life with the same level of overcommitment. You want to say yes to everything in this new place. You find yourself volunteering for extra tasks, offering to fix things you don't need to touch, inserting yourself into situations where you're not actually required. *This is withdrawal.*

You moved into a new house, but your nervous system is still convinced that the old, frantic, hyper-needed version of you is the only one who counts. It's not proof you made a mistake. It's proof you made a significant change, and your inner world is recalibrating. Like any detox, there will be days when you think, "Maybe I should just go back to how it was. At least I knew who I was there." Those are the days you remind yourself why you left. Not by beating yourself up, but by telling the truth: "I was tired of living in permanent emergency mode. I wanted a life where I was a person, not just a fire extinguisher."

The Voices You Brought With You. You may have left the building, but you brought the commentary. In the quiet moments of your new life, you start hearing a chorus. "You had something good and walked away.", "People like you don't make it doing this.", "You'll be back. You always come back.", "You're selfish for choosing yourself over the group."

"You're ungrateful. Do you know how many people would kill for what you left?" Some of these lines came out of the mouths of real people: a boss who didn't want to lose you, a family member invested in a certain image, a leader who took your leaving as personal disloyalty. Others are older. They sound like childhood messages about not being "too big for your britches." They sound like cultural scripts that say stability is always more virtuous than change. They sound like the version of you who learned, early, that stepping out was dan-

gerous. The fact that those voices are loud does not mean they are right. It does mean you have to decide what to do with them. One helpful move is to distinguish between the voice and the reality.

"That's my ex-manager's fear talking."

"That's my grandmother's value system, not mine."

"That's my 14-year-old self who didn't have options."

Then, gently, bring yourself back to the present: *"I am an adult, in this body, at this age, with these skills and experiences. I made this choice with more information than those voices had. I am allowed to learn in real time, not just in theory."*

You don't need to win an argument with the echo. You just need to stop letting it be the only narrator.

The Urge to Prove the Move Was Worth It. After a big decision, it's easy to feel like you're on trial. You imagine there is an invisible jury made up of your former colleagues, your family, your old friends, maybe your entire high-school graduating class, all watching to see what happens. So you feel pressure to perform your new life. You want the new job to be obviously better. You want the business to take off quickly. You want your social media to showcase constant wins. You want your face to look like "I have never been more peaceful" even on days when you're crying in your car between errands.

Underneath the performance is a fear: "If this doesn't look great quickly, maybe I really did mess up. Maybe they were right. Maybe I overestimated myself." In response, you might push yourself too hard. You might take on more in the new job than is wise, just to demonstrate that you're thriving. You might rush into a new relationship so you can show everyone (and yourself) that you're "over it." You might narrate your move to others as if it's already a finished success story instead of an ongoing, messy process. *But real change rarely offers instant, tidy evidence.* There is a middle stretch where things are uncertain, unglamorous, and un-postable. Where you haven't yet seen all the fruit of your decision, but you're too far from your old life to go back easily.

That in-between is not failure. It's transition. You don't owe anyone a perfectly curated story while you're still figuring out where the light switches are in this new house. You're allowed to say, "Some days I feel incredibly sure. Some days I'm scared. I still believe this was the right move."

When New Cheese Meets Old Habits. You can change the context and keep all your old habits intact. When that happens, your life slowly morphs back into the shape of the thing you left, just with updated wallpaper. You leave a workplace where saying "no" was basically forbidden, and in your new, healthier company, you still never decline anything. You overwork, burn out, and say, "See, it's always like this," when in reality, you brought your inability to set limits with you. You leave a church where disagreement was taboo, and in your new community—where people would actually welcome honest questions—you still keep your thoughts to yourself and then quietly complain that "no one really knows me here."

You leave a relationship where you were constantly walking on eggshells, and in your new relationship, you still edit every sentence so thoroughly that your partner only ever meets your polished representative and not your actual self. *New cheese does not automatically install new software.* If you don't examine your defaults, they will re-create the old dynamics in new environments. This can be depressing to realize. It can also be empowering: "If I am part of the pattern, I am also part of the solution."

You might notice, with a mix of humor and dread, "Oh, I'm doing that thing again—taking responsibility for everyone's feelings." Or, "I just volunteered for three extra committees, and no one even asked me to. That's not them. That's me." Instead of deciding, "Nothing ever changes," you can decide, "I have an opportunity here to respond differently in a place that might actually let me."

Building a Life That Matches the Reason You Left. When you moved, you had reasons. Maybe you wrote them in a journal. Maybe you told them to a trusted friend. Maybe you just felt them in your bones.

"I want to be able to breathe."

"I don't want to dread Sundays."

"I need to see my kids while they're still kids."

"I'm tired of hiding what I think."

Those reasons are not just poetic lines in the "why I left" speech. They are design instructions for the life you're trying to build now. If you left because you were exhausted, your new life has to include rest as a structural feature, not a reward you get once every six months. That might mean intentionally scheduling downtime, resisting the urge to fill every free evening, noticing when you start equating your worth with your output again.

If you left because you wanted more honesty, your new life has to include spaces where you actually tell the truth sooner. That might mean being more direct with your new manager, even when your voice shakes. It might mean letting your new friends see you when you're not "fine." It might mean catching yourself when you start to smooth over every conflict out of habit.

If you left to prioritize your health, your calendar needs to reflect that. Doctor's appointments, therapy sessions, exercise, sleep—these are not decorative extras. They are part of the architecture of the life you said you wanted. Big moves are upheld by daily patterns. If your days don't change, your years won't either, no matter what your email signature says.

Learning to Live With Other People's Opinions. One of the hardest parts of living with your new cheese is accepting that some people will never fully understand or approve of your move. They may respect it in theory but resent its impact on them. They may feel abandoned. They may feel judged. They may feel left behind. They may feel threatened by the idea that someone in their circle did something they themselves are afraid to try. Some will express their feelings directly. Others will go quiet. Some will make little jokes that land like jabs. Some will simply drift.

You might be tempted to spend a lot of energy managing their perceptions. You rehearse explanations in your head. You imagine the perfect conversation that would finally make them say, "Now I get it. I'm proud of you." You scroll their feeds, analyze their comments, and try to decode what they "really" think. The problem is, the more you orient your new life around their reactions, the less you're actually living your new life. There is a difficult, liberating shift that has to happen at some point:

- You stop basing the validity of your decision on how easily other people digest it.

- You don't have to be defensive. You don't have to be hostile. You can listen to what they say. You can even learn from parts of it.

But you start measuring your move less by their comfort and more by your own integrity. "Am I showing up in a way I respect? Am I being as kind as I can without lying? Am I willing to let some people be disappointed or confused so that I don't have to be disappointed and confused in my own skin? "Over time, people adjust. Or they don't. You can't build a future on the hope that one day everyone will clap. You can build one on the commitment that you will keep living in a way that you can look back on without flinching.

When the New Place Feels Ordinary (and That's Not an Insult). It's easy, before a move, to imagine the new chapter as endlessly exciting. You picture yourself waking up every day thrilled. You imagine work that feels like a constant adrenaline high. You imagine a relationship with zero awkwardness. You imagine a city that sparkles in every direction. *Then you get there.* You learn the commute. You learn the grocery store layout. The new job has mundane tasks. The new relationship has laundry and bills. The new city has traffic and bad weather and days when nothing particularly magical happens. You might start to wonder, "Did I really make all that effort just to… live a normal life somewhere else?"

Sometimes, yes. And that's not a failure. Part of living with your move is letting go of the fantasy that the "after" would be a movie montage. Real life, even good life, has a lot of Tuesdays. The question isn't, "Is every day thrilling?" It's more like, "Is my baseline experience of being myself in this life better than it was? Do I feel less cramped? Less on edge? More aligned, even when it's boring?" Ordinary can be a massive upgrade from chronically miserable. There's a particular peace that comes when you realize you can have a regular day in your new life and not secretly wish you were somewhere else. That's harder to post about than a big announcement, but it's the substance underneath the announcement.

Giving Yourself Permission to Be New. One of the kindest things you can do for yourself after a move is to let yourself be a beginner again.

This sounds obvious, but for high-functioning, competent, "I've got it" people, it's surprisingly hard. You were good at the old thing. You knew the systems. You had status. People asked for your opinion. You could do your tasks without checking the manual. You could walk through that building or that relationship or that community with your eyes half-closed and still hit all the marks.

Now you're new. You don't know all the unwritten rules. You're not the expert. You're not the default leader. You have to ask, "Where does this go?" or "How do we usually handle this?" You have to say, "I'm not sure yet." If your identity has been welded to competence, this can feel like a threat. You might be tempted to bluff. To pretend you understand more than you do. To over-commit so you can fast-track your way back to feeling essential. But newness is not a weakness. It's a sign that you are still willing to evolve. Saying, "I'm learning how I want to show up in this season," is more honest than trying to copy-paste your old self into a context that needs a different version of you.

You do not owe anyone the old level of over functioning. You do not have to bring every past persona with you. You are allowed to let some identities retire. Maybe you were the person who always stayed late. Maybe you were the unofficial therapist. Maybe you were the volunteer for everything. Maybe you were the one who never needed help. In this new life, you can experiment with being the person who goes home on time, who says, "I'm not the right person for that," who's part of the team instead of the engine, who asks for support before you collapse. *You moved your cheese.* You're allowed to move your self-concept too.

The Pull of the Old Maze. No matter how convinced you were that leaving was the right move, there will be days when the old life looks better in hindsight than it ever did in real time. *This is nostalgia's specialty.* You'll remember the camaraderie in the break room, not the panic in the restroom. You'll remember the nights out with your ex, not the nights you cried yourself to sleep. You'll remember the spiritual highs, not the spiritual manipulation. You'll remember the fun parts of the city, not the ways it quietly crushed you.

On a hard day in your new life, those memories will present themselves like a highlight reel and suggest, "Maybe you overreacted. Maybe you should go back." Before you start mentally packing, it helps to ask, "What exactly am I missing?" Is it truly the old job, or is it the comfort of being the expert again? Is it that specific relationship, or is it the feeling of being known, even if you were known in a role that hurt you? Is it that community, or is it the safety of being surrounded by people who already had a place for you? Those are genuine needs: competence, belonging, familiarity. But if you're not aware of them, you might misdiagnose the ache as, "I chose the wrong life," instead of, "I haven't built these elements into my new life yet." If you are considering going back—to a job, a person, a place—it's worth asking some pointed questions:

"What would have to be radically different for this to be healthy for me now?"

"Am I imagining returning there as the person I used to be, or as the person I am now, with new boundaries and clarity?"

"Am I thinking about this because I'm grounded and reflective, or because I had a terrible Tuesday and I want relief?"

Sometimes, people do go back in a new way, and it works. A company gets new leadership and the culture genuinely changes. A relationship ends, both people do deep work, and later rebuild something healthier. A person returns to their hometown with a new sense of self and engages differently. Other times, going back is just rewinding. Same dynamics, same roles, same unspoken rules, dressed up as a second chance. Only you—and often, someone wise outside the situation—can help discern which is which.

Making Peace With the Old Chapter. To live in your new life without constantly time-traveling, you have to make some kind of peace with the old chapter. Peace doesn't mean pretending it was better than it was. It doesn't mean pretending it was worse than it was. It means telling a full story. You might say, quietly, "That season shaped me. I learned skills there I still use. I met people there I still care about. I also tolerated things there that I'm not willing to tolerate anymore.

Both of those truths can stand." You might look at a photo from that time and allow yourself to feel warmth and sadness at once. You might acknowledge, "I was doing my best with what I knew then. I see more now. I'm allowed to adjust." You don't have to burn the old maze down in your memory to justify leaving it. You also don't have to turn it into a sacred monument you're not allowed to critique. You can bless parts of it and release the rest. "Thank you for what you were. You are not what I need now."

Becoming the Person Who Can Stay. The final piece of living with your new cheese is subtle: becoming someone who can stay in a healthier life without sabotaging it. If your nervous system is wired for chaos, peace will feel suspicious. If your identity is built on sacrifice, a sustainable pace will feel selfish. If you're used to being the background character in your own life, making choices that center your actual needs will feel unnatural.

So you practice. You notice when you start looking for new fires to jump into. You notice when you start minimizing your own progress. You notice when you feel the urge to undercut your joy before someone else does. And instead of reflexively obeying those impulses, you get curious about them.

"Why does this free evening feel wrong?"

"Why am I tempted to volunteer for three extra things I don't have capacity for?"

"Why do I feel like I need to apologize for being happier now?"

You won't catch it every time. You don't have to. Even catching it sometimes is a shift. Over time, you build tolerance for a life that is less frantic, less performative, more honest. You learn how to let good things last without constantly poking holes in them to prove you're realistic. You gradually accept that you are allowed to build something you don't have to escape from. That's when you know you're not just someone who can move your cheese. You're someone who can live with where you've put it. Not perfectly. Not without questions. But with enough presence that, on a random Tuesday, you notice you're not obsessing over the old maze or auditioning new ones. You're just here. Making coffee. Answering an email. Laughing at a text. Feeling a little tired, a little hopeful, a little human. And for the first time in a long time, that feels like enough.

CHEESE CHECK

This chapter is about actually living where you are now—emotionally, not just physically.

Take your time with these. *Name the "new cheese" you're living with right now.* A new job? Role? Season? Boundary? Relationship status? City?

Write: "Right now, my new cheese is ___________."

What do you miss most about your old life?

Be specific: people, routines, status, predictability, drama, being needed. Which of those needs could be met in a healthier way in your current season?

What old voices are still echoing in your head about this move?

Write 2–3 phrases you still hear. Next to each one, write a response from your present self.

Where are you secretly trying to "prove" this was the right decision?

Social media? Overworking? Overexplaining? *What would it look like to release that pressure, even a little?*

What new rhythms does this season invite?

List 2–3 small, practical habits that match who you want to be now. Pick **ONE** to commit to for the next 30 days.

When you're tempted to go back—emotionally or literally—*what do you forget about the old place?* Write three sentences that begin with:

"I tend to forget that back then I often felt ___________."

Write a short blessing that releases the old and welcomes the new.
For example:

"Thank you, old season, for ___________. I release you.

I welcome this new season of ___________, and I choose to be here."

You didn't move your cheese just to stand in the doorway of your new life, looking over your shoulder at the old one. You moved so you could live.

In the next chapter, we'll talk about relationships and community—how your moves affect the people around you, how to navigate shifting dynamics, and how to build connections that can handle the real you in every season.

CHEESE CHECK NOTES

Every friendship isn't meant

to go all the way to the finish line with you.

That doesn't make it fake.

It makes it finite.

Dr. Laide R. Alexander

CHAPTER NINE

When Your Cheese Move Shakes Your Relationships

Cheese never moves in isolation. Every time your life shifts—job, calling, boundaries, church, city, relationship status—the relational furniture around you shifts too. Some people: Celebrate you, support you, adjust with you and others; pull back, push back, or quietly disappear. You didn't just move your cheese. You moved the unspoken agreements people had with you:

- That you'd always be available
- That you'd always serve in that role
- That you'd always show up the same way
- That you'd always prioritize their comfort over your own growth

This chapter is about what happens to relationships when you start living differently—and how to navigate that without going back to shrinking.

People Who Loved the Old You. Most of us have people in our lives who loved a particular version of us: The always-on-call friend. The "strong one" in the family. The unpaid therapist or pastor for everyone's crisis. The reliable volunteer who never says no. The quiet spouse who never rocks the boat. The coworker who picks up the slack without complaining. When you change— when you rest, say no, move on, speak up, or step back—you are not just changing your life. You are changing their experience of you. *Some will adapt. Some will not.* You may hear:

- "You've changed."

- "You're not the same person anymore."

- "You used to be so humble/available/loyal."

- "Ever since you got that new job/degree/relationship, you're different."

Sometimes that's a compliment in disguise. Sometimes it's a protest. Either way, it reveals this truth: Not everyone who loved you, loved the real, or the evolving you. Some people loved the role you played in their lives. And when the role changes, the relationship has to either grow up or fade out.

The Difference Between Support and Control. After a big move, you'll quickly learn who was supporting you and who was controlling you. Support sounds like:

- "I may not fully get it, but I'm with you."

- "How can I help you in this transition?"

- "I trust you to hear from God / your own wisdom about your life."

- "If this doesn't work out like you hoped, you still have me."

Control sounds like:

- "I just don't see why you'd do that."

- "You're making a big mistake."

- "After everything we invested in you…"

- "So you're just going to leave us like that?"

- "If you go through with this, don't come back."

Support may ask questions, express concern, or even disagree—but it ultimately respects your agency. Control uses: Guilt, fear, shame, or ultimatums to keep you in place. Learning to tell the difference will save you years of emotional confusion.

When Your Growth Confronts Other People's Stagnation. Your move will sometimes act like a mirror to people around you. Your: New boundaries. New honesty. New courage. New pace. New self-respect. And can quietly expose where others are still: Overextending, people-pleasing, hiding, settling, avoiding their own decisions. Most won't say: *"Your growth is making me question my choices."* They'll say:

- "You're doing too much."

- "You think you're better now."

- "Everybody can't just up and change like that."

- "You've become selfish."

Sometimes, what they call "selfish," God and your therapist would both call healthy. You are not responsible for managing other people's discomfort with your healing. You are responsible for how you treat them in the process—but not for how they feel about seeing you free.

The Friendships That Don't Survive the Shift. Some relationships are for: A role. A season. A shared struggle. A shared environment (same job, church, neighborhood, stage of life). When one of you moves—physically, emotionally, spiritually—the shared ground shrinks. You might notice: Texts slow down, calls feel more surface, they don't ask about your new life, conversations stall around the "old days", you feel less and less like yourself when you're with them and it's tempting to: force the old closeness, overshare to keep them invested, dim your joy or growth so they won't feel left behind, but sometimes, the most loving thing you can do is accept:

> *"We were close for who I was then and where I was then. I bless that. And I release the pressure for this to look the same now."*

Every friendship isn't meant to go all the way to the finish line with you. That doesn't make it fake. It makes it finite. ***Finite can still be holy.***

Family: The Original Maze. Family systems are often the hardest place to hold onto a new you. You might be:

- The responsible one
- The quiet one
- The successful one
- The peacemaker
- The "problem"
- The one they all call
- The one no one calls until it's an emergency

When you move your cheese—change your boundaries, your availability, your role—the whole system wobbles. You might hear:

- "You think you're too good for us now?"
- "You're acting brand new."
- "We've always done it this way."
- "So now you're setting boundaries?" (with a tone)
- "You know how your mama/daddy/sibling is; just let it go."

You may feel pulled between: *Honoring your growth* and *playing your old part so the family doesn't get upset.* Here's a freeing truth: You can love your family deeply and still refuse to keep playing a role that harms you. Loyalty does not require self-betrayal.

Sometimes loving your family means:

- Not rescuing them
- Not joining the same arguments
- Not attending every event
- Not exposing yourself to the same harm
- Not letting their version of you be the only one that exists

You are allowed to become a healthier member of a system that may never change.

Romantic Relationships and "New You" Tension. When one person in a romantic relationship starts changing, it can feel threatening to the other. If you; start therapy, set new boundaries, change careers, deepen your spiritual life, heal from old trauma…your partner might feel: Inspired, intimidated, left behind, afraid you'll outgrow them, afraid of losing the version of you they know how to navigate. You may hear: "You're different now.", "You think you're better than me?", "So your therapist knows you more than I do?", "All this 'healing' is ruining our relationship." Or, if they're trying but struggling: *"I'm trying to adjust, but I don't know this version of you yet."* This is where communication matters. You can say things like:

"I'm not changing because I don't love you. I'm changing because I want to show up healthier—for me and for us."

"It's okay for you to grow too. I don't want to leave you; I want us both to be more whole."

"I know this is new. Let's get help together if we need it."

However, if your growth is consistently met with mockery, sabotage, or punishment, you may have to ask a harder question: *"Is this relationship compatible with the person I'm becoming?"* That's not a question to answer lightly or alone—but it's one you may need to face honestly.

Church, Ministry, and Spiritual Community. Few relationships get as tangled as those formed around church and ministry. When you: Step down, step away, change churches, change your theology, change your pace…you're not just changing a schedule. You're changing: How people see your calling. how they see your loyalty, how they see your faith. You might be treated as' a disappointment, a backslider, a rebel, a threat, a "cautionary tale", or you might simply experience the cold shoulder. It can feel like: "They loved my gift, not me", "I was family until I made a decision they didn't like", "Community was conditional".

That grief is real. If you're not careful, it can turn into: Bitterness, Cynicism, A vow to never trust spiritual community again. You don't have to rush back in. You may need a season of distance and healing. But over time, consider this: Don't let one unhealthy community convince you that you are destined to walk with God alone forever. Part of living with your new cheese may be learning how to: Find safer, healthier community, engage at a sustainable pace, be honest about your limits, refuse to confuse use with love.

Who Comes With You (and Who Doesn't). After a major move, you'll often discover three groups of people:

Travelers —They grow with you

They adjust to your boundaries.

They celebrate your growth, even when it inconveniences them.

They are willing to meet the new you, not just mourn the old one.

Visitors —They're in your life, but at a different distance

The relationship shifts: less often, more surface, or more defined.

You still care, but you no longer center their expectations.

You honor what you had without forcing what you no longer have.

History —They stay in the past

Not because you hate them, but because your paths diverged.

There's no active harm, just no active connection.

You can bless them without bringing them into every new room.

All three categories can be held without bitterness. Everyone isn't meant to be a Traveler. You aren't meant to be a Traveler for everyone, either. The key is to stop trying to drag History into the Traveler category.

How to Have Hard Conversations Without Begging. Sometimes, part of living with your new cheese is having hard conversations: With family about new boundaries, with friends about shifting expectations, with leaders about stepping down or leaving, with a partner about how your needs have changed. You are not responsible for convincing them you're right, getting them to fully understand or erasing all their disappointment. You are responsible for; Telling the truth as kindly and clearly as you can, owning your part without over-owning theirs, and not throwing grenades on your way out, if you can help it. You might say:

"I know this change affects you. I care about that. I also have to be honest about what I can and cannot keep doing."

"I value what we've had. My needs and capacity are different now, and I have to honor that."

"I don't expect you to fully understand. I do need you to respect that I've thought and prayed about this."

If they respond with: Manipulation. Character Attacks. Refusal To Hear You. …you've learned something important about how safe that relationship really was. That's painful information. It's also useful information.

Letting New People Meet the Real You. One of the gifts of a new season is that new people will meet you as you are now, not as you were. You don't have to:

- Pretend you're still the over functioning one
- Hide your boundaries until year three
- Downplay your story to make others comfortable
- Perform spiritual, professional, or emotional perfection

You can practice: Telling the truth about what you've been through (with discernment), saying "no" early instead of resenting people later, being honest about your limits from the start, letting people see both your strength and your healing. The more you do this, the more likely you are to attract relationships that can hold:

- Your calling
- Your humanity
- Your pace
- Your evolution

By the time the dust settles from a big move, it isn't just your calendar that looks different. Your relational map does too. Some people are closer. Some are farther. Some are just… gone. And then there's a fourth category: the people who are technically still there, but the air between you has changed in ways you don't quite have names for yet. The beginning of this chapter looked at the obvious tremors—family roles, friendships that don't make the jump, partners who feel threatened, spiritual communities that suddenly don't know what to do with you. Now let's talk about the subtler aftershocks. The second-wave effects. The stuff that shows up not in the first three months after your move, but two or three years later, when everyone thinks it's "old news" and you're still feeling the ripples. This is the part nobody puts in the testimony video.

The Politics of Your Move. Every relationship network—family, church, workplace, friend group—has a politics, even if no one calls it that. There are:

Unspoken hierarchies: who's "in," who's "important," who gets listened to.

Emotional alliances: who defends whom, who silently sides with whom.

Narratives: the official story about what it means to be "loyal," "strong," "humble," "wise."

When you move your cheese in a way that breaks one of those narratives, you don't just change your own storyline. You introduce a plot twist into everyone else's. You were the one who took whatever was handed to you at work. When you leave for a role that pays you what you're worth, it exposes that some people are still underpaid—but staying. That's political. You were the pastor's "right hand," the dependable volunteer who never said no. When you step back for the sake of your health, it quietly says, "Burnout is not a badge of honor." That's political. You were the sibling who always sent money home. When you set a limit, it surfaces the fact that others could contribute but haven't. That's political.

No speech required. Your move itself is the memo. Some people will thank you privately, even if they don't say it in front of others: "You leaving showed me I'm not crazy for wanting something different." Others will treat you like someone who broke the code. You may start to notice strange little behaviors:

People making a point of loudly declaring how "happy" they are to stay, as if answering a question no one asked.

Leaders suddenly preaching or talking more about "commitment" and "faithfulness," as if your departure were a morality play.

Friends dropping tiny comments like, "Well, not everyone can just go do what they want," with a smile that doesn't reach their eyes.

It's easy to internalize that and think, "I must have caused all this drama."

You didn't create the politics. You just refused to keep playing your assigned part in them. That refusal is disruptive. It's also honest. And honesty in a system built on quiet resentments will always look like trouble at first.

The Status Game You Didn't Know You Were Playing. When you move your cheese, you're not just changing where you spend your time. You're often changing your status—up, down, or sideways.

You may go from:

"Big fish in a small pond" to "one of many talented people in a bigger space."

"The pastor's favorite / CEO's right hand" to "new kid nobody knows yet."

"The one who stayed" to "the one who left," which, in some circles, is its own kind of scandalous status.

Status isn't just about titles and money. It's about where you sit in other people's imaginations.

You can feel the shift in small ways: The invites change. The tone of people's voices changes. The way they introduce you changes. In the old world, you were "our worship leader," "our director," "our star teacher," "our rising star." In the new world, you might just be "This is Jordan," full stop. That can be humbling, and if you're honest, a bit bruising. You didn't just lose a role; you lost a ready-made identity people affirmed on contact. On the other hand, some moves raise your visible status, and that comes with its own weirdness. You get the promotion. You get the platform. You get the degree, the bigger salary, the new title. People who were comfortable with you at one level now feel something they don't want to name: envy, inadequacy, a sense of being left behind. They might not say, "I'm jealous." They'll say things like:

"Must be nice."

"Don't forget us little people."

"Just wait, you'll see it's not all that."

You're suddenly managing another layer in your relationships: other people's projections about what your move "means." You can't fix that for them. You can, however, be honest with yourself about how much of your own discomfort is grief over lost status versus grief over lost connection. You're allowed to miss being known and admired. You're not required to go back to an ill-fitting life just to get that feeling back.

Money, Moves, and the Awkward Shift in Power. Many cheese moves come with financial implications, and money is one of the most quietly relational topics there is. You leave an underpaid but "noble" role for a corporate job that finally pays you well. Or you do the opposite: walk away from a lucrative role into something more aligned but less predictable. Either way, the money story changes. Suddenly:

You can afford some things your friends or family can't, and you feel guilty ordering what you want at dinner.

Or you can't do what everyone else does anymore, and you feel like the wet blanket who keeps saying, "That's not in my budget right now."

If you grew up in a context where money and morality were tightly braided ("rich people are greedy," "broke equals holy"), this can make your relationships… interesting. People may start making little comments about your choices:

"You're fancy now."

"You sold out."

"Must be nice not to have to worry about that anymore."

"Some of us don't have the luxury of doing what we love."

Underneath, there are often two things happening at once: Your financial reality really has changed. Their story about what that says about you has, too.

You can't control their interpretation, but you can be intentional about how you steward your new situation in relationships. Sometimes that means being more generous without being a walking wallet. Sometimes it means being honest: "I chose a path that pays me better, and that doesn't make me less committed to what matters to me." Sometimes it means letting go of the need to constantly prove you haven't "changed" just because your tax bracket did.

On the flip side, if your move involved a financial drop, you may feel a different kind of power shift. You might need help for the first time. You might be the one saying, "I can't do that this year." You might have to borrow or accept support. This can be humbling in families or friend groups where you were always the provider, the generous one, the one who paid without looking at the bill.

Your vulnerability may deepen some bonds—and strain others. Some people only knew how to relate to you as "the strong one." They don't know what to do with your need. They may avoid it. They may minimize it. They may offer advice when what you need is presence. Letting people see you in a season where your material life doesn't look impressive, but your inner life is becoming more honest, can be one of the bravest relational moves you make.

The Long Tail of "You've Changed". "You've changed" is one of the most emotionally loaded sentences in the language. Sometimes it's a simple observation. Sometimes it's an accusation. Sometimes it's both. In the first year after a big move, you hear it a lot. People haven't adjusted to the new you yet. They're startled. They're reacting. What's more interesting is what happens later.

Three years in. Five years in. Ten. You run into old acquaintances at weddings, funerals, reunions, random coffee shops. They say, "You've changed," with a mix of nostalgia and curiosity. The early sting is gone. You feel a different sensation: the strange, quiet pride of realizing, "Yes. I have. I'm not the person who could have tolerated that old life anymore." What used to feel like an accusation starts to sound like a simple fact.

Anyone who hasn't changed in ten years is either incredibly lucky or incredibly stuck. The longer you live with your new cheese, the more you realize that the sentence "You've changed" says at least as much about the speaker as it does about you. If they've also changed, it can be the start of a rich conversation: "We both grew. Let's compare notes." If they haven't, it can be a marker: "We took different paths. That's okay. We don't have to drag each other where we're going."

The question shifts from "How do I prove I haven't changed too much?" to "How can I honor who I was, while staying loyal to who I am now?"

When Your Move Becomes Other People's Excuse. One of the strangest outcomes of moving your cheese is when people use your story as a reason to not face their own. You'll hear things like:

"Not everyone can just leave like you did."

"Some of us don't have those options."

"You were always different, so of course it worked out for you."

On the surface, this sounds like realism. Underneath, it's often resignation disguised as fact. Sometimes they're right: your circumstances, privilege, timing, or support system did give you different options than they have. That's worth acknowledging. But sometimes they're using your uniqueness as a shield: "Because you had X, I don't have to seriously consider whether I could also change something." Your move becomes a kind of soothing story they tell themselves. "They're special. I'm not. Therefore, I'm off the hook."

You can't argue people out of their self-protective narratives. What you can do is tell the truth about your own limitations. You can say, "I didn't move because I'm fearless. I moved because staying became more expensive than leaving." Or, "I didn't do this alone. I had help, and it was still terrifying."

Sometimes, your honesty will open a tiny crack in their certainty. Sometimes it won't. Either way, your job is not to carry their excuses on your back. You didn't move your cheese to become a mascot for either "anything is possible if you just believe" or "only special people get out." You moved because you're a person, not a slogan.

The Quiet Relief on the Other Side. We've spent a lot of time on the loss and tension that comes with relational shake-ups. That's real, and it's important to name. But there's another side that doesn't get talked about as much: the relief. Relief when you realize the relationships that survived your move have more oxygen in them now. You don't have to censor yourself as much. You don't have to play the role as hard. You don't have to hustle for the same approval. Relief when you notice that some of the loudest critics have simply… faded. Their voices aren't in your ear every week. Their opinions don't loom as large. You didn't have to "win" them. Time just moved you into different orbits. Relief when you see your new boundaries actually working. The family member who used to call at 2 a.m. for every minor crisis starts texting first. The friend who relied on you for constant emotional labor finds a therapist. The workplace that expected unpaid overtime from you now has to hire another body because you won't quietly do two jobs anymore. *No one throws a party for those little shifts.* But they add up to a different felt experience of being you in your own life.

That's the point. Not to end up with a relational resume that looks impressive, but to create a relational ecosystem where you can exist as a whole person without constantly folding yourself into smaller shapes.

Becoming a Safe Place—for Yourself and Others. The last thing worth saying about moves that shake your relationships is this:

Eventually, you're going to be on the watching side of someone else's move. A sibling will set a boundary with the family. A friend will leave a job or a church you're still in. A colleague will say, "I can't keep doing this pace." A partner will start their own therapy journey and begin changing in front of you. You'll feel some of the same things other people felt when you moved:

fear, insecurity, maybe a flicker of jealousy, maybe the sting of, "If they change, what does that say about me if I don't?" In that moment, you'll have a chance to decide what kind of relational presence you want to be. You can be the person who says, "You've changed" like a sentence. Or the one who says it like a blessing.

You can reach for guilt and control. Or you can reach for curiosity and support, even when it costs you something. You don't have to be perfect at it. No one is. You just have to be honest enough to recognize, "This is bringing up my stuff," and kind enough not to make them responsible for fixing it.

The more you become a safe place for your own evolution, the more you'll be able to offer that safety to others. Not by never being affected by their moves, but by refusing to punish them for growing. That's how you start to form the kind of relationships that don't shatter every time someone picks up their cheese. They flex. They talk. They adjust. They grieve. They renegotiate. Sometimes they part ways. But they don't demand that anyone stay small to stay loved.

And if you've never really had that before, building even two or three of those connections might be the most radical relational move you ever make.

You don't need a thousand of those. A handful is life-changing.

CHEESE CHECK

This chapter is about facing how your moves have impacted your relationships—and how to live with that honestly.

Who most struggled with your last big move?
List 2–3 people or groups (family, partner, pastor, friends, coworkers).

What did they lose, or feel like they lost, because of your change?

Who genuinely supported you, even if they didn't fully understand?
Write their names.

How did their support show up (words, actions, presence, silence that felt like trust)?

Where do you feel the most pressure to "go back" to the old you for someone else's comfort?

With whom? In what ways? Complete this sentence:

"Around __________, I feel tempted to shrink by __________."

Which relationships are Travelers, Visitors, and History right now?
Put a few names in each category.

How does it feel to see them there, honestly?

Is there one hard conversation you've been avoiding since your move?
With whom? About what? What's one sentence you could say to start that conversation?

What new kinds of relationships do you need in this season?
Mentors? Peers on a similar journey? Safe spiritual community? Professional support?

What's one step you can take in the next 30 days to move toward that?
Write a short blessing over your relationships in this season. For example: May the people who are meant to walk with me now recognize me and I them. May I release with grace those who can't go forward with me. May I have courage to be fully myself with the ones who stay."

Your cheese moved. Your roles shifted. Your relationships are rearranging around that reality. You don't have to hold everyone the way you always have. You do get to choose, with more clarity and courage, who gets to walk with you in the maze from here.

In the next chapter, we'll talk about identity—who you are beyond any particular job, title, relationship, or role, and how to anchor yourself so that no matter where the cheese moves, you don't lose you.

CHEESE CHECK NOTES

If people constantly said: "

I don't know what we'd do without you."

"You're the glue that holds this together."

"You're always there."

It feels good…

until: you step away.

Dr. Laide R Alexander

CHAPTER TEN

Who Am I Without That Cheese?

At some point in this journey, a deeper question sneaks in: "If I'm not who I was there…who am I now?" Who am I without: That job? That title? That church? That relationship? That ministry role? That version of "strong" I always had to be? When a big piece of your life shifts, it can feel like your whole identity has been erased. You don't just lose a role. You lose a ready-made answer to, "So, what do you do?" or "Who are you to them?" or "Where do you go?" This chapter is about rebuilding a sense of self that can survive any cheese move.

The Old Badges You Used to Wear. Most of us walk through life wearing badges—visible or invisible labels that tell us (and others) who we are. Badges like: "Doctor", "Pastor", "Leader", "Mom / Dad", "Breadwinner", "The Responsible One", "The Talented One", "The Strong One", "The First in the Family to…" Badges can be beautiful. They can reflect real achievement, calling, and service. The trouble comes when the badge becomes bigger than the person. You don't know who you are without it. You tolerate harm just to keep wearing it. You confuse the badge with your worth. When that badge is taken away—or you lay it down—it can feel like being stripped in public. You may think:

- "What do I matter now?"

- "Who am I if I'm not that anymore?"

- "If I'm not useful in that way, will anyone still want me?"

Those questions are painful. They are also an invitation.

Role, Season, and Self: Learning to Separate Them. One way to regain your footing is to separate three layers:

ROLE —What you do

Job titles, ministries, family responsibilities, positions.

SEASON —Where you are right now

Student, caregiver, in transition, healing, building, resting.

SELF —Who you are underneath all of that

Your values, temperament, wiring, gifts, story, essence.

When your cheese moves, usually it's your role and season that change first. But it can feel like you have been erased. Try this: *"I used to be Director of X. That was my role, not my whole self."* Or *"I'm in a between season right now. This is a season, not a life sentence."*

"Underneath both, I'm still someone who values ___________, is wired for ___________, and cares deeply about ___________. That is my self."

Roles will come and go. Seasons will rise and fall. The self—that deeper "who"—can grow, but it doesn't vanish.

When Your Worth Was Tied to Being Needed. One of the hardest identity crashes happens when your worth was tied to being:

- Needed.
- Impressive.
- Useful.
- The answer.
- The fixer.

If people constantly said: *"I don't know what we'd do without you." "You're the glue that holds this together." "You're always there."* It feels good… until: You step away. You can't show up like that anymore. Or you realize they loved your function more than your full self. Suddenly: No one's calling. No one's asking. The calendar is quiet. And the question becomes: *"If I'm not urgently needed, am I still valuable?"* **Yes.** You were never meant to live as a 24/7 emergency response team. You are not only worthy when you're exhausted, overbooked, or rescuing someone. Your value is not in how indispensable you are to other people's chaos. It's in the fact that you are a person—with a soul, a story, and a future—not a tool.

Grieving the Old You Without Staying There. There is a version of you that fit that old season perfectly:

- The you who could pull all-nighters and bounce back
- The you who believed certain doctrines without question
- The you who thought that relationship was forever
- The you who could tolerate more than you can now
- The you who loved being at the center of everything

You might miss them. You might think: "That me was stronger." "That me was more spiritual." "That me was more confident." "That me didn't need therapy." But remember: That version of you didn't know what you know now. They didn't see what you've seen. They hadn't carried what you've carried. They hadn't outgrown what you've outgrown. You can honor them without going backward. Try saying:

"Thank you to the me who got me through that season. I don't have to be you anymore. I'm allowed to evolve."

Grief for an old self doesn't mean that self was better. It just means they were familiar.

Listening for the You Underneath the Noise. If your identity has been wrapped around roles and expectations for a long time, the quieter question is: ***"Who am I when no one is asking me for anything?"*** To answer that, you may need to: Turn down the volume of constant doing, Step away (for a while) from spaces that only see you as what you provide, Sit in uncomfortable stillness long enough to hear your own voice again, Ask yourself:

- When no one is watching, what do I naturally gravitate toward?

- What kind of conversations light me up?

- What injustices or needs break my heart?

- What environments help me breathe deeper?

- What kind of work makes time move faster—in a good way?

- What kind of work makes time drag?

These aren't just preferences. They are clues to your wiring. Your real identity is less about "I am a title" and more about:

"I am someone who values…"

"I am someone who is drawn to…"

"I am someone who cannot stand to see…"

"I am someone who feels most alive when…"

Identity and Faith: More Than What You Do for God. If faith is central to you, another layer of identity often needs healing: ***"Who am I to God if I'm not doing all the things I used to do?"*** When you step back from serving, leading, or carrying spiritual responsibility, you might feel: Less "used" by God. Less "important" in the Kingdom. Less sure of your place. You may confuse: Calling with busyness, Anointing with visibility, and Obedience with overwork. But consider:

- The God who loved you before you ever did anything "for" Him

- The God who calls people into hidden seasons as often as public ones

- The God who rested on the seventh day—not because He was tired, but to set a rhythm

Your identity in God is not: "I am what I produce." "I am the ministry I lead." "I am the number of people who need me." It's more like: *"I am a beloved person who gets to participate in what God is doing—not a machine God runs until it breaks."* **Sometimes, the holiest thing you can rediscover is that you matter even when you're not "on."**

The Temptation to Grab a New Costume. After losing one identity, you'll be tempted to quickly grab another: New title. New relationship. New platform. New theology you wield like a weapon. New "brand" of yourself online. Anything to avoid feeling naked. Be careful. If you rush to define yourself by the next thing, you'll just trade one costume for another. You'll say: "I'm not that anymore; now I'm THIS." And the cycle repeats: Attach. Over-identify. Outgrow. Collapse. Scramble for a new label. Instead, consider a slower path:

- Try on new roles without marrying them.

- Let yourself experiment without needing each experiment to become your whole identity.

- Allow your description of yourself to be longer than one sentence.

You are more than a headline.

Rewriting Your "I Am" Statements. Pay attention to the sentences that begin with: "I am just…", "I am the kind of person who always…", "I am not someone who can ever…"These are identity anchors—sometimes helpful, sometimes harmful. For example:

- "I am just a support person, not a leader."

- "I am the one who always holds everyone else together."

- "I am not someone who can start over at this age."

- "I am the messed-up one in my family."

- "I am nothing without my work."

Where did those come from? A parent's words? A pastor's sermon? A boss's evaluation? A partner's criticism? Your own fear? You don't have to pretend they never affected you. But you also don't have to let them be the last word. Try gently revising them: From *"I am just a support person"* to *"I am someone who supports well—and I am also capable of leading when called to." From "I am the one who always holds everyone together" to "I am someone who cares deeply, but I am not responsible for everyone's survival." From I am not someone who can start over" to "I am someone who finds starting over scary and possible."* Subtle shifts. Big impact.

Building an Identity That Can Travel. The goal is not to build an identity that only works in one maze. The goal is to build an identity that can travel with you through many. Ask:

- Who do I want to be regardless of my role?

- What kind of person do I want to be known as in every room?

- What values do I want to carry into any job, relationship, or city?

Words like: Honest. Courageous. Kind. Curious. Grounded. Faithful. Discerning. Creative. Joyful. Wise. These are portable identities. You can be honest: As a CEO or as an intern. As a married person or a single person. In your hometown or a new country.

You can be courageous: Leaving or staying. Speaking up or staying silent in wisdom. Starting something or ending something. The more your "***I am***" is rooted in how you live, not just where you live or what you do, the less any single cheese move can undo you. There's a particular kind of silence that shows up after a big move. The logistics are over. The emails have been sent, the keys returned, the pictures taken down. Your calendar looks suspiciously empty in places that used to be full. The adrenaline wears off. And into that quiet steps a question that is less about schedules and more about existence:

"If I'm not who I was there… who am I now?"

Who am I without that job everyone knew me for?

Who am I without that title that did half my introductions for me?

Who am I without that church, that city, that relationship, that ministry, that version of "strong" I performed for so long?

It can feel less like "I made a change" and more like "I got erased."

You didn't just hand in a badge. You lost a ready-made answer to, "So what do you do?" and "Who are you to them?" and "Where do you go?" And in a world that loves quick labels, not having one feels like showing up to a formal dinner in pajamas. This chapter isn't about how to get a shinier badge faster. It's about how to rebuild a sense of self that can survive any cheese move—one that isn't permanently welded to whatever maze you happen to be in at the moment.

When Your Name Tag Did All the Work. If you've ever worn a literal name tag with a title under your name, you know how convenient it can be:

"Hi, I'm Jordan —Director of X."

"Hi, I'm Dr. So-and-So."

"Hi, I'm Pastor / Minister / Elder / Lead Something."

"Hi, I'm Mom to three boys."

"Hi, I'm the First in My Family to…"

You don't have to explain yourself. The tag does it for you. People slot you into a mental category: smart, successful, spiritual, responsible, accomplished, safe, impressive. Even without the physical sticker, most of us walk around with internal badges: The Talented One. The Breadwinner. The Strong One. The Reliable One. The One Who Made It Out. Badges aren't inherently bad. They often reflect real labor, sacrifice, care, calling. The trouble starts when the badge grows larger than the person wearing it. You start to feel like you are the role. You put up with things that hurt you because you're afraid of losing the identity that comes with the job, the relationship, the ministry, the reputation. You forget there was a "you" before anyone handed you that label.

Then something shifts. You leave. Or you're laid off. Or you burn out. Or you age out. Or you change your mind. Or life simply happens. The badge falls off. And suddenly, you feel oddly naked in rooms where you used to feel important. You catch yourself thinking, "What do I matter now? Who am I if I'm not that anymore? If I'm not useful in that way, will anyone still want me around?" Those are not shallow questions. They are the doorway to a deeper kind of identity than the kind you can pin to a blazer.

The Day After the Title Disappears. One of the strangest experiences in life is the first time you introduce yourself after a big identity-anchoring role is gone. You're at a party or a conference or a family event. Someone asks the most socially acceptable intrusive question: "So, what do you do?" And there's this tiny pause where your brain reaches for the old script and comes up empty. "Oh, I used to…" you start, and then realize you don't want your entire existence to be framed in the past tense. But you also don't have a neat, new noun that feels big enough to explain the mess of "I'm in between things right now and trying not to panic."

If you're used to impressive answers, this can feel like a fall from grace.

A friend of mine, let's call her Alicia, went through this after leaving a high-profile role at a well-known nonprofit. For years, "I'm Director of…" had been her elevator pitch. People's eyes would light up. They'd say, "Oh wow, that's amazing," and she'd feel that little hit of "I'm doing something that matters." Then she left. On purpose. For good reasons. Reasons her therapist applauded, and her doctor quietly said, "Finally." Two weeks later, she was at a neighborhood barbecue. Someone new turned to her and asked, *"So, what do you do?"* She told me later, "I felt like someone had unplugged my personality. I heard myself say, 'I'm… between things,' and wanted to disappear into the potato salad." The job had changed. Her calendar had changed. But what really rocked her was realizing how much of her self she had outsourced to that title.

It wasn't just about work. It was about worth. That's what this identity work is really about: how to exist as a person when the external markers that once told you who you were are gone, or different, or no longer fit.

When Your Value Was Measured in Emergencies. Some identities are flashy: doctor, CEO, pastor, founder. Others are quieter but just as consuming: the glue of the family, the person everyone calls first, the one who always knows what to do, the unofficial counselor, the human Swiss Army knife. If you've lived most of your life as the person others depend on, you know the mix of pride and exhaustion that comes with it. People say things like, "I don't know what we'd do without you," and "You're the only one I can talk to," and "You're the one holding all this together." It feels good. It also quietly trains your nervous system to equate "being needed" with "being valuable."

Then, for whatever reason, the dynamic changes. You're no longer in that environment. You set new boundaries. You move. You burn out and can't keep showing up the same way. You simply decide, "I cannot continue to be everyone's 24/7 emergency response team." The calls slow down. The texts decrease. People find other people. There's relief. And then there's an ache. You look at your quieter phone and wonder, "If nobody urgently needs me, do I still matter? If I'm not solving everyone's crisis, who am I?" This is one of the most disorienting identity withdrawals there is. It's not just about missing the people. It's about missing the feeling of being the vital organ in every body you're attached to.

And yet, if you zoom out, you might also notice this: the version of you who was constantly propping up everyone else was running on fumes. That person got sick more. That person had less room for their own feelings. That person's "strength" was often just a refusal to fall apart in public, even when it would have been human to do so. You can honor that version of you—they did what they needed to do to survive certain seasons—without deciding that's the only version you're allowed to be. There is a kind of worth that exists even when your phone is on "Do Not Disturb." You were always more than the sum of other people's emergencies.

Missing the Old You (Without Making Them a God). There's another layer to identity grief that doesn't get talked about much: grieving the old you. Not just the job, not just the relationship, not just the community.

The self who fit there.

The you who could pull all-nighters and bounce back with three hours of sleep and a coffee.

The you who believed certain ideas without wrestling.

The you who thought a particular relationship or institution was forever.

The you who could tolerate drama and chaos without flinching because you didn't yet know the cost.

The you who took certain risks because you hadn't learned how much it hurts when they don't work out.

You might look back at that person with a mix of fondness and frustration.

"Wow, they were naïve."

"Wow, they were brave."

"Wow, they put up with so much."

"I miss how confident they seemed."

"I miss how certain they were."

It's tempting, on hard days, to idealize them. "That me was stronger. That me was more spiritual. That me didn't need therapy. That me could handle everything I'm dropping now." But that version of you didn't know what you know now. They hadn't carried what you've carried. They hadn't seen what you've seen. They hadn't reached the limits you've now hit. You can be grateful for them. You can even borrow some of their energy when you need it. What you don't have to do is regress. You are not obligated to go back to an older operating system just because it ran fast, if you now know it was also corrupting your files. There's a simple practice here that can be surprisingly powerful:

> *"Thank you to the me who got us through that season. You did the best you could with what you had. I don't have to be you anymore. I'm allowed to be someone new."*

Grief for an old self doesn't mean that self was better. It just means they were familiar.

The Terrifying Question: Who Am I When No One Needs Anything?. If your sense of self has been wrapped around roles and expectations for a long time, the quietest, scariest question is not, "What will I do next?" It's, "Who am I when no one is asking me for anything?"

When there are no urgent emails.

When your kids are with someone else.

When your calendar isn't full of meetings, rehearsals, services, practices, obligations.

When you're not prepping for Sunday or Monday or the next big thing.

A lot of people discover, in that silence, that they're not sure what they actually like. They know what they're good at doing for others.

They know what gets praised. They know what's expected. But if you ask, "What do you genuinely enjoy when no one's watching? What conversations make your eyes light up? What problems do you naturally lean toward solving? What environments make your shoulders drop an inch?"—you might get a blank stare. Answering those questions often requires a kind of stillness that feels wildly unproductive. You might have to temporarily step away from spaces that only interact with you as a role. You might have to say no long enough for the noise to die down. You might have to sit on your own couch on a Saturday and resist the urge to immediately schedule something so you don't have to feel bored. It will be uncomfortable.

You might feel lazy. You might feel selfish. You might feel, frankly, a little lost. But in that space, if you stay with it, small clues start to surface. You notice you keep reaching for certain kinds of books or shows or podcasts. You notice that time moves faster when you're solving particular types of problems and drags when you're doing others. You notice you're oddly energized after some conversations and drained after others. You notice there are topics you always circle back to, injustices you can't let go of, kinds of beauty you're compulsively drawn toward.

Those aren't just quirks. They're signals.

Your real identity is less "I am a title" and more "I am someone who values this, is drawn to that, comes alive doing this, cannot stand that." Titles can be taken. Wiring tends to stick.

When God, Work, and Identity Got Tangled. If faith has been a big part of your story, there's a special kind of identity confusion that can happen when you stop doing all the things you used to do "for God."

You step back from serving or leading. You change churches. You stop being the person who's always on the stage or always in the background holding up the stage. You realize that a lot of what you called "calling" was actually compulsion, or people-pleasing, or fear of disappointing a leader. And suddenly, without the constant activity, you're left with a disorienting thought: "Who am I to God if I'm not doing all that?"

Even if you theologically "know" that your worth isn't in your work, your body may have been trained differently. Your nervous system might equate busyness with being loved, visibility with favor, exhaustion with faithfulness. You might feel less "important" in the Kingdom because fewer people see your name on a schedule. You might doubt your closeness to God because you're not living on caffeine and spiritual adrenaline anymore. There is a version of faith that treats you like a machine: as long as you're producing, you're valuable. When you stop, you're replaced.

There is another version that treats you like a person: loved before you ever did anything remotely useful, invited into seasons of hiding and healing as much as seasons of public work. If you've only ever known the first kind, stepping back from constant doing can feel like falling off a cliff in your relationship with God. It might help to remember that rest isn't a glitch in the design of a human life. *It's part of it.* Your identity in God—if that language matters to you—is not "I am what I produce for God." It's closer to "I am someone God knows by name and story, not by job description." That doesn't answer every practical question, but it does loosen the chokehold of "If I'm not on, I'm nothing."

Trading Costumes vs. Being a Person. There's a reflex most of us have after an identity collapse: grab a new costume as fast as possible. You leave the job and immediately throw yourself into a new one, partly because you need income, but partly because you cannot bear the feeling of not having a polished answer to "So, what do you do?" You step away from one kind of religious space and immediately adopt a new label, a new camp, a new "tribe" to belong to, complete with merch and talking points.

You exit a relationship and almost instantly slip into another, not necessarily because you're ready, but because being "half of something" feels more legitimate than being alone at the table. You pivot from one brand of "strong" to another: from overworking for God to overworking on healing; from being the martyr in your family to being the savior in your friend group. It's understandable. Being in between identities feels like being socially unemployed.

But if you simply swap one rigid badge for another, you'll recreate the same problem with a different aesthetic. You'll attach. Over-identify. Outgrow. Collapse. Scramble for the next thing. A slower, more terrifying, more honest path is to allow your description of yourself to be longer than one sentence for a while.

"I'm someone who's finishing a long chapter and not entirely sure what the next one is yet."

"I'm exploring a few different directions and trying to pay attention to what actually fits."

"I'm rebuilding my life around being a person, not just a role. It's… a work in progress."

You don't have to say all that to everyone at the barbecue. But you can say it to yourself. You can treat new roles as experiments instead of forever homes. You can let yourself try things without needing each thing to be "it." You can resist the urge to turn every new interest into a brand, every new insight into an identity.

You're not a headline. You're a whole article.

The Stories You Tell Yourself About Yourself. If you listen closely to your own thoughts, you'll notice certain sentences that start with "I am…" and end with a small, heavy cage.

"I am just a support person, not a leader."

"I am the one who always holds everyone else together."

"I am not someone who can start over at this age."

"I am the messed-up one in my family."

"I am nothing without my work."

Where did those lines come from?

A parent's offhand comment.

A teacher's criticism.

A pastor's sermon that confused humility with self-erasure.

A boss who needed you to stay small.

An ex who weaponized your worst moments and called them your nature.

Your own fear, repeating itself until it sounds like fact.

These "I am" statements are powerful, not because they're true, but because you've rehearsed them. You don't have to pretend they never shaped you. But you can challenge their monopoly. Instead of trying to swing to the opposite extreme—"I am a world-changing leader and everyone else is wrong about me!"—you can make subtler, truer edits.

"I am someone who supports really well—and I'm also capable of leading when it fits."

"I am someone who cares deeply about people, but I'm not solely responsible for everyone's stability."

"I am someone who finds starting over scary and possible."

"I am someone with a messy history, not 'the messed-up one' like it's a job title."

"I am someone who values meaningful work, but I am not my job."

Those may sound like small changes. They're not. They're like moving a train track by a few inches; you don't see much difference in the first mile, but you end up in a completely different place.

Identities That Can Travel. One of the goals of this whole cheese-moving journey is to build an identity that can travel with you. Not a fragile one that only works if you have this job, that relationship, that level of visibility, that community. *A portable self.*

Think of the people you admire most, up close, not on stage. Chances are, what you respect about them isn't their specific role. It's their way of being. You might describe them with words like:

Honest.	Kind.
Courageous.	Grounded.
Curious.	Joyful.
Steady.	Wise.
Creative.	Fair.

These are not titles. *They're traits.*

You can be honest as a CEO or as an intern, as a parent or as someone without kids, in your hometown or on the other side of the world. You can be courageous leaving a job or staying to finish a hard project. You can be courageous ending a relationship or staying to rebuild it in a healthier way. You can be kind with a microphone in your hand or in a hospital waiting room with no spotlight anywhere.

When you start rooting your "I am" in the kind of person you're becoming, rather than the specific stage you're currently on, your life gets less fragile. Jobs can change. Titles can come and go. Churches can split. Relationships can shift. Kids grow up. Algorithms tank your reach. Trends move on. A self built on "I fight for what's right even when it costs me," or "I tell the truth as kindly as I can," or "I show up as fully human, not just as a role," is a self that can follow you into any maze. That doesn't mean you won't grieve each change. You will. It does mean no single cheese move gets to erase you.

The Awkward Middle: When Your Old Life Is Gone and the New One Isn't Built Yet. There's one more piece of this identity puzzle that deserves its own spotlight: the in-between. The season where your old roles are over, your old badges are off, and the new shape of your life is… not clear.

You might be:

In career limbo, between jobs or pivoting industries.

In relational limbo, post-breakup or post-divorce or redefining what family looks like.

In spiritual limbo, not where you were, not yet sure where you're going.

In geographic limbo, back in your childhood home or in a temporary living situation or in a new city that doesn't feel like yours yet.

In those seasons, identity work isn't theoretical. *It's Tuesday.*

You're filling out forms that ask for your occupation and staring at the blank line longer than you should.

You're attending an event alone for the first time in years and wondering who, exactly, walked through the door.

You're answering, "How are you?" with, "Depends on the hour."

The temptation in the awkward middle is to define yourself against what you left.

"I am not that anymore."

"I will never do that again."

"I'm done with those kinds of people, places, roles, beliefs."

Sometimes that's necessary. Boundaries often start with "no more of this." But if you only ever define yourself by what you're not, your identity will always be a reaction, never a creation. The work of this chapter—the deep, slow, quietly revolutionary work—is to start answering a more constructive question:

Given everything I've seen, lost, learned, survived, and outgrown... who do I want to be now?

Not in the abstract. Here. In this apartment, this city, this body, this bank account, this particular web of relationships, this moment in history. Who do I want to be in the way I answer emails? In the way I talk to the barista? In the way I respond when my family pushes my old buttons? In the way I treat myself on the days I'm least impressive? You may not have a neat title for that person yet.

That's fine. Titles can wait. The person wearing them cannot.

CHEESE CHECK

This chapter is about meeting yourself again—without the old badges and costumes.

List 3–5 badges you've worn in the past. Titles, roles, family positions, reputations. Next to each, write: "This was a role, not my whole self."

____

____

____

____

____

Finish this sentence honestly:

"The identity loss that hurts the most right now is losing being _________."

What did that identity give you (respect, certainty, belonging, control, purpose)?

Write down 3 "I am" statements you've been carrying that might be too small or too harsh. Then rewrite each one with more truth and more compassion.

When no one needs anything from you, what do you naturally enjoy or care about? List at least 3 activities, topics, or causes.

What do these reveal about your deeper wiring?

If your job/role disappeared tomorrow, what parts of you would still be there?

Skills, values, ways of relating, faith, personality traits.

Circle the ones you want to lean into more in this season.

Write a short identity statement that doesn't mention a title or role. For example:

"I am someone who is learning to live honestly, love deeply, and create spaces where people can breathe." Keep it rough; you can refine it over time.

Bless the old you—and release them. One or two sentences:

"Thank you to the version of me who ___________. You got me here. I release you with love and choose to grow into who I am now."

Your cheese will move again in this life—jobs, seasons, roles, even beliefs may shift. But you don't have to fall apart every time the scenery changes.

There is a "you" that is deeper than any maze, any title, any room.

The rest of this journey is about learning to walk with that you—so that wherever the cheese goes next, you can go with yourself, not instead of yourself.

CHEESE CHECK NOTES

Pause and name it:

"I am tired because I have been adapting for a long time."

That's not weakness.

That's an honest inventory

of what your body, heart, and mind have carried.

Dr. Laide R. Alexander

CHAPTER ELEVEN

When the Cheese Moves Again

Just when you start to settle into a new season—new job, new boundaries, new city, new you—life taps you on the shoulder and says: "We're moving the cheese… again." The opportunity you thought would last? *Restructured.* The relationship you rebuilt carefully? *Shifts.*

The stability you finally felt in your body? Interrupted by illness, loss, or change. The identity you just finished unpacking? Invited to grow… or to let go. You may feel: *Tired. Angry. Confused. Embarrassed* ("I thought I was done with this."). Afraid ("What if I can't do another transition?"). This chapter is about repeat movement—what to do when life won't stop rearranging the maze, and how to walk through multiple shifts without losing your mind or your hope.

"Not Again" Fatigue. There's a particular exhaustion that comes with repeated change. You might think:

- "I just got here."
- "I just rebuilt."
- "I just healed from the last one."
- "I'm too old for this."
- "Why can't my life just be normal for a minute?"

Change fatigue can show up as:

Numbness —"Whatever. I don't even care anymore."

Cynicism —"Nothing ever works out."

Hyper-vigilance —"I can't relax; something bad is always coming."

Self-blame —"This keeps happening, so it must be me."

Pause and name it: *"I am tired because I have been adapting for a long time."* That's not weakness. That's an honest inventory of what your body, heart, and mind have carried.

The Difference Between a Spiral and a Circle. When the cheese moves again, it can feel like you're back where you started. Same feelings. Same fears. Same kind of loss. You might say: *"I thought I already learned this lesson.", "Why am I here again?"* Here's a helpful picture: A circle goes around and ends where it started. A spiral passes similar territory… but at a different level. From the ground, a spiral staircase just looks like you're going in circles. From the side, you can see you're actually rising. Ask yourself:

- "What's the same about this change as last time?"
- "What's different about me this time?"

Maybe this time: You're more honest. You ask for help sooner. You set boundaries faster. You don't abandon yourself. You grieve in real time instead of after the fact. *That's not a circle. That's a spiral.*

You Are Not Starting From Scratch. When the cheese moves again, it's easy to feel like all the work you did before has been erased. It hasn't. You've gained:

- ***Skills***
  Communication, planning, boundary-setting, self-awareness

- ***Wisdom***
  What you will and won't do again, what red flags mean, how your body speaks

- ***Tools***
  Therapy language, coping strategies, spiritual practices, supportive contacts

- ***Receipts***
  Actual memories of "I made it through last time"

You are not the same person who faced this kind of shift five or ten years ago. You might tell yourself: *"I've never been here before as this version of me."* Same type of storm, different boat.

Checking Your Old Narratives. When things shift again, old internal narratives like to wake up. They say:

- "See? You're unstable."
- "You can't keep anything."
- "You always mess it up."
- "God must be punishing you."
- "You're cursed."
- "You're too much / not enough."

Before you agree, ask: *Who taught me to explain life this way? Does this story match what actually happened, or just how it feels? What evidence do I have against this story?* For example:

Narrative: "I always mess things up."

Reality check: Some things ended because of your choices. Some ended because of other people's choices. Some ended because life changed (economy, illness, timing). You have also made choices that saved you and others.

More honest statement:

"I have made mistakes and also made wise moves. I am still learning, not doomed." You don't need a fairy-tale story. You need a truer one.

Stabilizing Yourself When Nothing Else Is Stable. When external cheese keeps moving, you need internal anchors. Ask, "What can I stabilize while everything else is shifting?" Think in three layers:

Body Anchors

Small, repeatable actions that remind your nervous system: "We're still here."

- Regular sleep and wake time (as much as possible)

- A simple movement routine (walk, stretch, breathe)
- Eating at least one actual meal sitting down
- One grounding practice: deep breaths, short prayer, a few minutes outside

These are not "nice extras." They are survival rails.

Heart Anchors

Practices that give your emotions somewhere to land.

- Journaling, voice notes, or talking with a trusted person
- Naming feelings instead of judging them ("I feel scared," not "I'm stupid for feeling scared")
- Allowing tears, frustration, and confusion without rushing to fix them

A short daily check-in question: "What do I need today—comfort, courage, clarity, or connection?"

Hope Anchors

Perspectives or practices that remind you your life is bigger than this moment.

- Scriptures, affirmations, or phrases that have held you before
- Remembering past seasons where you couldn't see a way and one opened
- Visualizing not a perfect future, but a possible one: "Six months from now, it is possible that…"
- Staying connected to at least one person who can hold hope when you can't

Stability is not "nothing ever changes." Stability is "something in me knows how to stand, even when things move."

When It's Time to Release the Old Plan. One of the hardest parts of repeated change is letting go of the plan you thought you had. "I was supposed to be there for 20 years." "We were supposed to grow old together." "This was supposed to be my forever church / career / city." When reality refuses to follow your script, you can: Keep clutching the script and resent your life or Start writing a new page with trembling hands. Grieving the old plan might sound like: "I really thought it would look different. I loved that picture. I'm sad it didn't happen that way." You don't have to pretend you're "unbothered." But once you name the loss, you can also ask: "Given what's real now, what kind of life is still possible?" "What dream needs to be buried—and what dream needs to be revised, not canceled? ***Some dreams die. Some dreams change clothes.***

Guarding Against "Why Bother" Thinking. After multiple disruptions, "why bother" thinking creeps in:

- "Why love if it might end?"
- "Why commit if jobs are unstable?"
- "Why plan if life is going to change it anyway?"
- "Why heal if something else will just break me?"

Underneath is a longing for guarantees. But life was never offering guarantees—only opportunities:

- To love, even without a contract on the outcome. To build, even knowing storms exist.
- To rest, even when tomorrow is uncertain.
- To grow, even if growth won't protect you from all pain.

You might reframe: From: *"Why bother if it might not last?"* To: *"Is it worth it, even if it doesn't last forever?"* Many of the most meaningful things in your life were temporary:

- Seasons.
- Friendships.
- Roles.
- Moments.

They still mattered.

Learning Your "Change Profile". Not everyone experiences repeated change the same way. It helps to know your change profile: *Do you tend to rush into the next thing to avoid discomfort? Do you freeze and wait until the last minute, hoping it will all go away? Do you over-research and never actually decide? Do you hand the decision to someone else?* Look back at previous transitions:

- What did you do that helped you?

- What did you do that made it harder?

For example:

Helping patterns:

- Reaching out for support early

- Giving yourself permission to feel sad and scared

- Making a simple, realistic plan

Hurting patterns:

- Ghosting people instead of communicating

- Burning bridges in anger

- Pretending you were fine until you collapsed

- Overcommitting to prove your worth in the new place

Knowing your tendencies lets you say: *"Okay, this is a change season. I know my usual traps. I'm going to choose differently where I can."*

Permission to Pace Yourself. When the cheese moves again, you may feel an internal drill sergeant:

- "Hurry up and adjust."

- "You don't have time to feel."

- "Figure it out now."

- "You should be over this already."

But transitions have phases, not just moments. Roughly:

Shock / Disruption —"What just happened?"

Emotion / Grief —"This hurts / scares / angers me."

Meaning-Making —"What does this say or not say about me, God, others?"

Experimenting —"What small steps can I try in this new reality?"

Integration —"This is part of my story now; I know how to live here."

You might move back and forth between phases. That's normal. Pacing yourself means not demanding Step 5 peace while you're still in Step 1 shock, letting yourself be in transition without calling yourself a failure, or celebrating small signs of integration as they come.

When You're Afraid You Won't Survive Another Move. For some, the fear is literal: "Will this stress break my body?" "Will this grief break my mind?" "Will this loss break my faith?" If you're here, take this seriously. You may need:

- **Professional help** (therapy, medical support, spiritual direction)
- **Practical support** (financial advice, community resources)

A plan to reduce unnecessary stress while you navigate what you can't control. It is not a lack of faith to say: "This is too much for me to carry alone." If you can, tell at least one safe person: *"I'm not okay, and I need help."* Your past resiliencc is not infinite. You are allowed to upgrade your support system as life keeps moving.

When the Maze Has Politics (and You're in the Middle). By the third or fourth major shift, you discover something nobody mentioned in the TED talks about "navigating disruption."

The maze has politics.

Not just office gossip or who gets invited to which meeting. The deep politics of: who pays for each move, who benefits, and who gets to pretend they had nothing to do with it. If you're a CEO or senior leader, you live at the intersection of several competing realities every time the cheese moves:

- Investors or boards who want efficiency, returns, and a story that plays well on calls.

- Employees who want stability, dignity, and a reason to keep giving you their best hours.

- Customers or communities who want continuity and trust.

- Your own family, who would like to see you occasionally not thinking about all of the above.

On paper, you're supposed to "balance stakeholder interests." In real life, you're often choosing whose life gets harder this quarter. You'll never see that sentence in a leadership competency model, but it's true. Over multiple moves, those choices add up. They become your actual record, whether or not you ever put them in a slide.

There was a founder I'll call Denise who led a global services firm. Over a decade, she steered through three major strategic overhauls. Each time, the easiest path would have been to protect the people with the biggest titles and let the cost roll downhill. She decided, very early, on a different rule: in any major change, the people with the most power and pay would absorb visible cost, too.

That meant executive pay freezes when they had to freeze hiring. It meant re-scoping her own role and perks before asking others to tighten belts. It meant saying "no" to a deal that would've doubled the valuation in the short term but gutted the workforce in the process. It slowed some things down. It also meant that when the cheese moved for the third time, her people didn't just hear "we're all in this together" as a slogan. They had a decade of receipts.

Repeated change exposes whether your organizational politics are just buzzwords or an actual ethic. You don't get to control the maze. You do get to decide which direction the sharpest edges point. That's power. Not the title. Not the car. Not the corner office. The power to decide who bleeds when you cut.

If that sounds dramatic, sit with it. Because if you don't face that reality consciously, you'll eventually drift into the default setting of every system: preserve the top, outsource the pain. And you'll call it "tough but necessary decisions," while wondering why your best people quietly stop trusting you.

The Public Version of You vs. the Person Who Goes Home. For most people, a bad quarter is a bad quarter. For you, it's a headline. Or at least a rumor. By your third major change, you have a public persona whether you wanted one or not. You are:

The leader who "bet big and won."

The leader who "overreached and had to retreat."

The leader who "cut deep to save the company."

The leader who "stayed too long."

The leader who "left too early."

Pick your flavor. The narrative machine will choose one.

Meanwhile, you're still the same person who goes home and argues about dishes, worries about your kids' grades, and forgets where you parked. The dissonance between the public you and the actual you gets louder with each move. After the second or third turnaround, there's a risk you'll start living like a character in your own case study. You become a little too aware of how your decisions will look in the eventual podcast interview. You start telling stories in the present tense that are already edited for future consumption. You ask yourself, "Will this look decisive?" instead of, "Is this actually right?" There's a term in medicine: *iatrogenic harm*—damage caused by the treatment itself.

There's an identity version of that in leadership: narrative-ogenic harm.

It's when the story you're telling about yourself starts driving your behavior more than the truth of the moment. One leader I worked with, we'll call him Theo, was famous in his industry for a bold restructuring that saved a legacy brand. Articles were written. Panels were moderated. He became "the guy who's not afraid to swing the axe." Two years later, when the environment changed again, he found himself instinctively reaching for the same playbook.

"People expect me to make the hard call," he told me. I asked him, "Do you expect that of yourself because this is actually the right move, or because you're used to being the one who swings first?" After a long silence, he admitted, "I don't know. I like being that guy. But I'm not sure the company needs that guy right now." That's the danger of leading multiple big moves: you can get addicted to the version of yourself that looks best on paper and lose sight of the version your current reality actually requires.

The antidote isn't to stop telling stories. It's to keep a few people in your life who are profoundly unimpressed by your résumé. People who will ask, "Okay, but how are you?" and won't accept "Busy, but good," as an answer. People who knew you before the titles, or who don't care about them now. If there is no room in your life where the public narrative can be put down and examined, you will eventually confuse "my brand" with "my soul." And when the cheese moves again, you won't just be protecting your people or your company. You'll be protecting your mythology. That never ends well.

The Invisible Invoice of Each Decision. Every big move generates an invoice. Not the kind your CFO tracks. The kind your body, your relationships, and your people quietly keep. The late nights you normalized as "just a season" that somehow lasted three years. The birthdays you missed with a promise to "make it up later." The staff who stayed through two restructurings and are now watching you plan a third with a look you can't quite read. You don't get those for free. Most leaders underestimate the lag on these invoices. The costs don't show up right away. Your team might rally in the first layoff. They might even rally in the second reorg, out of loyalty to you and each other. By the third, something else appears: a subtle, quiet recalibration of how much of themselves they're willing to bet on your next promise.

It doesn't mean they're disloyal. It means they're human.

They've seen enough to know that every "we're turning a corner" speech might be followed by another curve. On your side, you might not feel the cost until your kid makes a joke that lands too hard: *"We should put your picture on a milk carton: 'Have you seen this parent?'"*. Or your partner stops bothering to remind you about the thing you keep missing, because it hurts less to not expect you than to be let down again. Or your doctor looks at your lab results and says, "What's your stress level like?" in that careful voice that means "It's higher than this chart says is safe."

None of this makes you a villain.

It does mean you're running a deficit that no performance bonus will cancel out. The point is not to tally every sacrifice and spiral into guilt. Guilt without action is just self-centeredness in a different outfit. The point is to start asking a sharper question as the cheese keeps moving:

"Is the way I'm absorbing and distributing this change sustainable for the people around me, including me?"

Not "Can I handle it for one more quarter?" You've proven you can do that. The question is, "If I keep doing it exactly like this for three more years, what breaks?"

Not in theory. Specifically.

Your sleep? Your marriage? Your senior team? Your sense of purpose? Leaders often think of risk in terms of markets and competitors. Repeated transition teaches you to think of risk in terms of human limits. Ignore those, and the maze may technically stay standing—while everyone inside slowly burns out.

You included.

Time Horizons: When Every Quarter Feels Like Sudden Death. One of the subtlest effects of repeated change is how it distorts your sense of time. After enough "urgent" pivots, everything starts to feel like a sprint. Every quarter feels existential. Every metric is a cliffhanger. Every board meeting is a verdict. Short-term thinking stops being a temporary posture and becomes a permanent lens. You can feel it in your planning:

You stop asking, "Where do we want to be in five years?" because you're not sure what planet you'll be on in five months.

You quietly drop investments that only pay off later: deep training, mentoring, succession, systems that would make things easier but won't impress anyone this year. You make hiring decisions based on who can plug a hole today, not who can grow the organization tomorrow.

It's understandable. It's also dangerous. Because someone is always thinking long-term. If it's not you, it'll be a competitor, a new entrant, or the people who take over once you're too tired to keep playing sudden death.

The challenge is not to pretend you're in a stable world when you're not. It's to hold two clocks in your head at once. One that says, "We have to make payroll next month." And one that says, "Five years from now, what will we wish we'd started now, even in the middle of this?"

A leader I'll call James took over a mid-size company that had been in permanent firefighting mode for years. Every six months, there was a new "critical initiative." Every year, a new theme. The staff could recite them the way kids recite old cartoon jingles.

James did something small and strange in his first all-hands. He said, "I'm going to be here for at least five years, if you'll have me. I don't know exactly what the world will throw at us. But I do know there are certain things we will keep doing no matter what: building people, improving how we work, and telling the truth about where we are. Those aren't projects. They're non-negotiables."

Then he backed it up.

Even in two rough years, they still set aside time and money for development. They still ran post-mortems where people could speak freely. They still invested in systems that didn't "pay back" within the quarter. It didn't make the storms go away. It did start to lengthen the organization's time horizon.

People stopped flinching at every new idea, because not everything was treated like a fire drill. They began to trust that some things would endure across moves. As a leader, you can't manufacture stability. You can decide which few commitments will outlast any single disruption, and act accordingly. That's long-term thinking in a short-term world. Not a five-year plan set in stone, but a five-year spine you refuse to break, even when the cheese is on wheels.

Successors, Shadow Selves, and Letting the Next Person Move the Cheese. One of the cruel ironies of leadership is that just when you've finally learned how to lead through change without destroying yourself, it might be time to hand the maze to someone else.

Succession isn't just a governance issue. It is an identity issue.

If your sense of self has been tightly braided with "I'm the one who gets us through," imagining someone else in that role can feel like planning your own obsolescence. You start thinking in unhelpful binaries:

Either I stay and we survive, or I leave and it all falls apart.

Reality is rarely that dramatic. But your ego is.

There's also a quieter, less talked-about dynamic: your shadow successor. This is the version of the next leader you carry in your head—the one who will either vindicate your choices or expose them.

If they keep your strategies, you feel right.

If they reverse them, you feel wrong.

If they succeed, you feel replaced.

If they fail, you feel guilty for leaving or secretly satisfied that you were needed.

You haven't even met them yet, and they're already living rent-free in your psyche. I watched this play out with a founder—call him Malik—who led his company for twenty years, through every imaginable storm. When the board finally pushed for a succession plan, he agreed in theory. In practice, every candidate was "not quite right." Too aggressive. Too cautious. Too corporate. Too green. Too different. Underneath, Malik wasn't just evaluating them. He was defending his identity.

"If I pass this on and they change direction, what does that say about what I built?"

"If they keep everything the same, what does that say about their own leadership?"

"If they move the cheese in ways I wouldn't, will that be an insult to my tenure?"

It took him a long time to realize that he was trying to hire a successor who would keep the maze frozen in the shape that proved he'd been correct.

That's not succession. That's taxidermy.

Healthy succession accepts three uncomfortable truths:

The next leader will move the cheese in ways you wouldn't.

Some of those moves will improve on what you did.

Some will mess things up you worked hard to build.

All three can be true while your own contribution remains real and meaningful.

Your legacy is not how well the next person imitates you. It's whether you leave the place capable of surviving being led by someone who is not you.

That means:

Systems that don't require your personal heroics to function.

A culture that doesn't treat disagreement with you as treason.

A team that has practiced making significant decisions without your hand on every lever.

If you've led through multiple moves and everything still relies on your presence to hold, that's not just a sign of how strong you are.

It's a sign of how fragile your organization is. And it's a warning that the bravest cheese move you may ever make is the one where you step aside.

Not after a scandal.

Not after a collapse.

Not after you're exhausted and bitter.

But while you're still clear-eyed enough to bless the next season, even if it doesn't look like the one you would have chosen.

When the Maze at Home Is Also Shifting. The world tends to talk about leadership as if your life happens in layers: first work, then "personal," with a neat line in between. *Repeated change has a way of setting that line on fire.*

You're closing a plant the same year your oldest leaves for college. You're raising capital while your partner is quietly wondering if they still recognize you. You're negotiating a merger the same month a parent's health takes a hard turn. You're selling the company at the exact moment your own body starts issuing ultimatums. These aren't distractions. They're the other half of your reality. There's a subtle cruelty in the expectation that you'll treat them as side quests—something to "manage" around the "real" work of leading.

In truth, the maze at home and the maze at work share a nervous system. If you've been through several upheavals in both, you eventually hit a moment where you realize: "I cannot keep pretending these are separate lives." So you start having different kinds of conversations. Not just, "I'm going to be busy this quarter," but, "If I say yes to leading this next move in the way they're asking, here's what it will cost us. Is that a trade we're actually willing to make?"

You invite your family, or whoever your core people are, into the discernment, not just the fallout. You stop announcing decisions as faits accomplish that everyone else has to work around. This doesn't mean outsourcing your choices to your partner or kids or friends. It means recognizing that your leadership is not a solo sport played off to the side of your "real life." It's one of the main ways your life touches theirs.

A founder I'll call Elena turned down a very prestigious "fix-it" role at a global company. On paper, it was perfect: huge scope, huge comp, huge platform. The kind of offer you're supposed to say yes to and then humble-brag about by saying, "After much thought and prayer, I've accepted..."

She and her spouse sat down one night and did something different. They wrote out—not on a slide, just on paper—what the last two major moves had cost their family: the missed events, the nights of single parenting, the constant low-grade tension of living with someone half-present. Then they asked, "Are we willing to go through that again for this? Not in theory. Us, now, in this house, with these kids at these ages?"

The answer, to their surprise, was no. Not because they were afraid. Because they were done pretending those costs were incidental. That "no" didn't make Elena less of a leader. It made her a leader whose definition of success had finally widened enough to include her own life.

Humor as a Survival Skill (Not a Distraction). If you've noticed that the only people laughing in serious meetings are the ones who've been through several of them, that's not an accident. There's a kind of humor that's just avoidance— deflecting, minimizing, refusing to face reality. There's another kind that's a pressure valve. It says, "We see the absurdity. We're not pretending this is normal. We're going to tell the truth, and we're going to survive it."

In organizations where the cheese moves a lot, gallows humor often shows up first in the middle ranks. They make jokes about the naming conventions for the "new initiative" every year. They give nicknames to the conference rooms where the big decisions are always announced. They meme the corporate jargon before the ink dries. If you're not careful, as a senior leader, you'll interpret this as disrespect. Sometimes it is. But often, it's a sign that people are metabolizing change the only way they can without screaming.

As a CEO, your relationship to humor in repeated change seasons says a lot about your internal freedom. If you can't laugh at any of it—not the absurd timing, not the mismatch between slogans and reality, not your own past misreads—you're probably carrying more than your share of the world on your back. If you only ever laugh at other people's expense—competitors, regulators, "the field," your own staff—you're probably using humor as a shield to avoid facing your part. The healthiest leaders I've seen through multiple moves can do three things:

Laugh at themselves without collapsing into self-contempt.

Laugh with their people, not just at them.

Know when it's time to stop joking and name the grief.

In a town hall about a tough downsizing, one CEO started by saying, "I know some of you have a running bingo card for how many times we can say 'strategic realignment' in one meeting. I promise, we're going to speak like humans today. You can put the bingo cards away." The room laughed. Then he followed it with, "What we're talking about is going to land differently for each of you. For some, this will be painful news. For others, it'll be a relief. My job is to make sure we don't hide behind language that makes it sound like this is happening to spreadsheets instead of people." *That's humor as an entry point to honesty, not a detour from it.*

When the cheese keeps moving, a well-placed, self-aware joke can be a way of saying, "We're still here. We haven't turned into robots. We can see the absurdity and still do the work." You need that. Otherwise, the only two modes left are deadly serious and dead inside.

One Leader, Ten Years, Many Mazes. Stories are easier to believe than principles. So instead of more abstract insight, let's follow one leader through a decade of moving cheese. Not a superhero. Not a villain. Just someone recognizably human who keeps having to redraw their map. We'll call him Daniel.

When we meet him, he's 42, recently promoted to CEO of a mid-sized tech company you've never heard of unless you work in that niche. No beanbag chairs. No rockets. Just boringly important software that keeps other businesses running.

On his first day, his assistant shows him the office. "This used to be a library," she says. "Now it's yours." He looks around at the shelves, mostly empty, and thinks, "I should put some books here so I look smart." That's his first leadership decision: optics over function. A small, harmless one. But it sets a tone.

Year 1–2: The Glory of the First Move. The board didn't hire Daniel to keep things as they were. They hired him to "modernize the business," which is code for "change things without making us look stupid. "The maze is already starting to wobble: new competitors, new tech, customers grumbling about the old product. There's money in the bank, but the trend line is gently sloping in the wrong direction.

Daniel does what good CEOs do in case studies. He listens. He visits offices. He asks questions like, "What's one thing we should stop doing?" People are pleasantly surprised. His predecessor mostly spoke in monologues. He finds the obvious early wins: a clunky approval process that everyone hates, a product line they've been keeping on life support out of sentimentality, a leadership meeting that has 18 people and no decisions. He trims, tweaks, and announces a new direction with charts, conviction, and just enough humility.

It works. Revenue stabilizes. A couple of projects he backed early pay off. Industry press writes a flattering profile: "Quiet Operator Steadies Legacy Firm." At home, his spouse jokes, "Should I get used to living with a genius?" He laughs, slightly too loud. Because part of him believes it. Not that he's a genius, exactly. But that he has a feel for the maze. That he can see three moves ahead. That this is what he was made for.

He buys nicer suits. He fills the office bookshelves. He starts to answer "How's it going?" with "Busy, but good," in the tone of someone who is slightly in love with their own busyness.

If the story ended here, he'd be a tidy success story. But then we'd have a pamphlet, not a book.

Year 3–4: The Move He Didn't Choose. In year three, a much larger company takes an interest. They don't want to buy his firm outright. They want a "strategic partnership," which is corporate for "we'd like the parts of you that help us, without your problems." The board is intrigued. They see access to new markets, new distribution, new prestige.

Daniel has concerns, but he also has a mortgage, kids with braces, and a board member who keeps reminding him that "this could be your legacy." The deal goes through. On paper, it's a win. Stock bumps. People clap in town halls. The slide templates get updated with the new partner's logo. Underneath, the maze is being quietly rewired. Decisions that used to be local now have to go through "alignment calls." The product roadmap gets edited to fit someone else's priorities.

His people sit in meetings where they're politely told what's "strategic" now, and it's often whatever helps the larger partner's quarterly story. Daniel spends his weeks on planes and video calls, explaining his company to people who never quite learn how to pronounce its name.

At home, his spouse stops joking about living with a genius and starts saying things like, "We see you on Instagram panels more than at dinner." He rolls his eyes at that—internally, of course. He's not that reckless. "It's just a season," he says. "Once this settles, it'll calm down."

It doesn't. The partnership drags on his team more than it lifts them. Projects are delayed waiting for joint approvals. Good people leave because they're tired of being "the smaller brand" in every room. In year four, the larger company has its own crisis and quietly pulls back. The "strategic partnership" shrinks to a much less glamorous vendor relationship. The board meetings get awkward. Someone asks, "Did we overextend? Should we have stayed independent?"

That someone is not Daniel.

He's thinking the same thing, but the question feels radioactive. To say it out loud would be to admit that his first really big move might have been, at best, a mixed bag. He says instead, "We learned a lot. We're better positioned now." It's not a lie. It's just not the whole truth.

Year 5: The Move That Costs Him People. By year five, the market has shifted again. A scrappy competitor has eaten their lunch in a key segment. Their old product still prints cash, but less each year. The board wants a "bolder response." This time, Daniel doesn't need convincing. He's restless. The partnership years left a bad taste. He wants a move that's clearly his.

He backs an internal skunkworks project: a new platform that would leapfrog their current offerings. He moves high-performers onto it, starves some legacy work to fund it, and bets his next few years of credibility on its success. He announces the initiative with all the usual phrases: "transformational," "future of the company," "all-in." His people follow. They work nights. They cut corners where they can. They ship a first version that is, in truth, not ready.

Customers are polite at first. Then they are not. Support tickets spike. Social media gets testy. The sales team quietly starts selling more of the old product again, because it works. Inside the company, a split emerges. Some people back the new vision. "We have to move forward." Others feel like second-class citizens, keeping the lights on while the "cool kids" break things.

Daniel sees the tension and does what many CEOs do when their beautiful new idea is wobbling: he doubles down. He entangles his identity with the project's success. He starts hearing any criticism of the initiative as criticism of him. When a long-time engineering leader raises concerns about the timeline,

Daniel says, "We can't be afraid of change." The words are right. The tone isn't. The leader leaves six months later. *Others follow.*

By the end of year five, the new platform is limping along. It's not a failure, exactly, but it's not the leap they promised the market or themselves. The board is nervous. The staff is tired. The brand is a little bruised.

In a rare moment of honesty with a friend over coffee, Daniel says, "I think I broke something. Not just the product. The trust. I pushed too hard."

His friend says, "So fix it."

He says, "I don't know how." What he means is, "I don't know how to fix it without admitting, in front of everyone, that I got carried away." He goes back to the office and starts working on a "course correction" memo that somehow makes the whole thing sound like an inevitable phase of innovation.

It's very well written. It is also the document his successor will later read and call "the point where we started losing people."

Year 6–7: The Move Forced by the Numbers. Markets don't care about your feelings. In year six, a combination of bad timing, external shocks, and their own missteps catches up with the company. Revenue dips harder. Their cash cushion shrinks. Credit terms get tighter. The board's tone changes from "What's our strategy?" to "What's our survival plan?"

This is the move Daniel truly didn't want to make: significant layoffs. He has done small trims before. Performance issues. Role consolidations. Quiet exits. This is different. This is "we cannot afford this many people" territory.

The finance team brings options. Charts. Ratios. Comparables. They're not heartless. They're trying to give him choices. Every version has the same shape: a lot of names. For the first time in his career, Daniel feels physically ill in a budget meeting. He knows, in his head, that there are worse options. If they do nothing, everyone loses their job eventually. If they act now, most people can stay.

He also knows, in his heart, that no amount of "greater good" rhetoric will pay someone's rent when they're the one cut. He sits in his car after the board votes and has a thought he's never let in before: "I don't want to be the person who signs this." Not "I don't want to do this." "I don't want to be this."

But the signatures are his to give. He does the right things, outwardly. He works with HR to offer as much severance as they can. He insists on telling people in person, not by email, even though it's excruciating. He refuses to let the blame be outsourced to "the board" or "the economy." He stands in front of the remaining staff and says, "This was my call. I hate it. I also believe it's what gives us a real chance to be here a year from now."

It is, by any reasonable measure, a responsible performance of a brutal role. It also takes something out of him that does not grow back in the same way. At home, he is quieter. His spouse notices he stares at nothing for long stretches. He starts waking up at 3 a.m. for no reason he can articulate. He tells no one at work that he's thinking, for the first time, "Maybe I'm done." Not done today. Not in a dramatic way. Just… nearing the edge of whatever reservoir he's been drawing from. But the company stabilizes. The numbers improve.

The board, relieved, starts talking about "the next chapter." *He nods.* Inside, something in him is already writing an ending.

Year 8: The Move He Makes for Himself. In year eight, nothing explodes. No scandal. No sudden market collapse. No hostile takeover. From the outside, it looks like a good year. They launch a solid new product—not category-defining, but respectable. Employee surveys tick up a little. They're not a rocket ship, but they're not sinking.

Inside, Daniel feels like someone who has finished a marathon and knows there is no medal at the finish line. The thought he had in year six returns, clearer: "I don't want to be this anymore." Not "I don't want to lead." He still cares about people and problems and building things. But he no longer wants to be the person at the exact center of every maze shift. The one whose nervous system is expected to absorb every tremor.

He starts, quietly, to imagine a future where someone else is in his office. Where he is in a different role, or a different field, or just at home for dinner more often. He feels guilty for even thinking about it. Leaders are supposed to be tireless. Or at least to pretend. He wonders if he's "burned out." He reads an article about burnout and rolls his eyes at the list of symptoms, which he recognizes too many of, and then keeps reading.

He thinks about talking to the board, then imagines their faces and can already hear the lines: "Now? When we're finally stable?" "You can't leave right as things are turning." "Think about your legacy." He thinks about talking to his spouse, then remembers all the times he's said, "Just one more push," and how those pushes always seemed to multiply.

He does something else instead. He calls an old mentor, someone who has no stake in his current job. Over coffee, he says, "I think I'm done."

The mentor doesn't say, "No, you're not." He doesn't say, "You can't walk away from this." He doesn't say, "Think of the money." He says, "Okay. Done when? And done how?" Those two extra words—when and how—turn a vague ache into a real plan.

They spend two hours sketching out what a responsible exit might look like: shoring up the team, naming and training a successor, communicating well, leaving before he's hollow. It will take time. But for the first time in years, Daniel feels less like a man being dragged by events and more like someone making an actual choice.

He goes home and tells his spouse, "I think I'm going to leave in about two years. Not run away. Land the plane, then get off." His spouse looks at him for a long moment and says, "I was wondering when you'd let yourself say that."

Year 9–10: The Move That Redefines Him. The next two years are the strangest of his career. He's still CEO. He still signs contracts, approves budgets, deals with crises. But he's also quietly working himself out of a job. He starts pulling back from being the bottleneck in every decision. He stops inserting himself into every high-stakes meeting.

He names, privately at first, then publicly, a small group of leaders he sees as the future. He gives them real authority, not just fancy titles. He also starts telling the truth in board meetings he would previously have spun. When someone says, "We should think about a new five-year plan with you at the helm," he says, "That's not realistic. We need to talk about succession. I'm not burned out. I'm not leaving next week. I am, however, not going to be here forever, and we should behave accordingly." The room goes very still. Someone asks, "Is there a problem we don't know about?" He says, "No. That's the point. I'd like to do this before there is."

It is, in its own way, the boldest move he's ever made. Not because he's sacrificing himself for the company. Because he's refusing to sacrifice himself to the company. He works with the board on a formal plan. It's messy. There are egos. There are politics. There are people who had assumed they were the obvious successor and are not thrilled to find out otherwise. He navigates all that with a level of calm that surprises him. The man who once entangled his entire identity with a single product launch is now able to say, "This decision will outlast me. That's exactly why I shouldn't be the only one making it."

At home, his kids are older. They're half-interested in what's happening at work, mostly interested in whether he'll be at their games. He is. Not at all of them. But at more than before.

On his last official day as CEO, the company throws a tasteful event. People give speeches. Someone makes a slide deck of "Daniel through the years" with questionable hairstyle choices. He says a few words. They're fine. The real ending, for him, happens later that night, when he walks into the office alone to clear the last of his things. He stands in front of the old library shelves, now full of books he actually read, and feels… not triumphant. Not devastated. Just done.

He thinks about the partnership he would do differently. The product he pushed too fast. The people he hurt without meaning to. The layoffs that still visit him at 3 a.m. some nights. He also thinks about the people who grew under his watch. The customers who wrote in unprompted to say, "You made our work easier." The colleagues who found their voice in meetings he once dominated. He realizes his life, over ten years, has become something no case study will capture: a series of imperfect decisions made by a fallible person trying, on most days, to do more good than harm.

He turns off the light, leaves the key on the desk, and walks out. The next morning, someone else sits in that chair.

The cheese will move again. He will read about it in the news or hear about it from friends. He will have opinions. But for the first time in a decade, he will not be the one tasked with explaining it to everyone else. He will be just another person in the maze of his own next chapter.

That, more than any title he ever held, may be the truest test of who he has become: Can he live a life where his worth is no longer indexed to how many people depend on him to move their cheese? Ten years in, through wins and bruises and late-night spreadsheets and early-morning flights, he has earned the right to find out.

And so have you.

CHEESE CHECK

This chapter is about facing repeated change with more honesty and less self-condemnation.

Name the cheese that just moved (or might be about to).

Job? Health? Relationship? Ministry? Finances? Sense of calling?

Write: "Right now, what's shifting is ___________."

Where do you feel "not again" fatigue in your body and mind?

Tension? Numbness? Irritability? Brain fog?

Complete: "My body is telling me it's tired by ___________."

Compare this to a past change. What's similar? What's different? How are you wiser or better resourced now than then?

Write down one old narrative that tries to wake up when things change.

"I always ___________" / "I never ___________."

Gently rewrite it into a truer, kinder sentence.

Identify one body anchor, one heart anchor, and one hope anchor for this season.

Example: walk after dinner (body), 10-minute nightly journal (heart), one verse/phrase you return to (hope).

What part of your old plan do you need to grieve?

Write 2–3 sentences starting with:

"I really thought ___________. I'm sad that ___________."

Name one way you will choose to move through this change differently than last time.

Asking for help sooner? Not ghosting? Resting more? Planning more?

Write it as a commitment:

"This time, I will ___________."

Your cheese may move again. More than once. But every time it does, you have the chance to respond with a little more clarity, a little more compassion for yourself, and a little more wisdom than before.

> ***You are not just surviving the maze.***
> ***You are learning how to walk it with your eyes open.***

CHEESE CHECK NOTES

There will be people you love deeply who simply cannot

or will not go where you're going.

Not because they're evil.

Not because you're better.

Because your paths diverge.

Dr. Laide R. Alexander

CHAPTER TWELVE

When You're the One Moving Someone Else's Cheese

Up to now, we've focused on what happens when your cheese moves—by life, by others, or by your own decisions. But there's another side to this story: Sometimes you are the one who moves the cheese for other people. By:

- Leaving a role they counted on you to fill

- Ending a relationship they thought would last

- Changing a boundary they benefited from

- Stepping into a new calling that reorders the team, family, or ministry

- Growing in ways that mean you no longer fit the version of you they built their expectations around

You're not just someone whose life has been rearranged. You are also someone whose growth, obedience, or limits will rearrange other people's lives. This chapter is about holding that reality with honesty, compassion, and courage—without collapsing into guilt or becoming careless.

When Your Yes Feels Like Their Loss. You might be in a season where:

- Your yes to rest means your family has to do more.

- Your yes to a new job means your team loses your presence.

- Your yes to therapy means your partner can't ignore issues anymore.

- Your yes to boundaries means your church or ministry can't lean on you the same way.

- Your yes to healing means your friendship no longer revolves around mutual dysfunction.

Your internal dialogue might sound like:

"I know this is right for me, but I hate that it hurts them." "I feel selfish even though I'm not trying to be." "If I were stronger, maybe I could keep everyone happy." "I wish there was a version of this where nobody had to lose anything." There usually isn't. Every real yes has a shadow cost for someone. The goal is not to find a cost-free yes. The goal is to steward your "yes" with integrity and love.

The Guilt That Shows Up When You Grow. When you start to change, guilt can show up in sneaky ways:

Survivor's guilt —"Why do I get to have this opportunity when others don't?"

Boundary guilt —"Who am I to say no when they're used to my yes?"

Prosperity guilt —"Is it okay for me to be blessed when some of them are still struggling?"

Clarity guilt —"Now that I see what was unhealthy, I feel bad for ever participating."

Guilt can be:

- Healthy, when it points to something you genuinely need to own or repair.

- Misplaced, when it punishes you simply for changing, healing, or receiving.

Ask your guilt:

"Are you here because I actually did harm?" If yes, we'll deal with that. "Or are you here because I'm breaking an old, unspoken rule that kept me small?"

You don't owe your old rules your life. You do owe people honesty and care as you change.

Owning Impact Without Owning Everyone's Emotions. When your move impacts others, there are two ditches:

- **Over-ownership** —"Everything they feel is my fault."

- **Under-ownership** —"That's their problem; I don't care."

Healthy ownership sounds more like: "My decision is mine. Its impact touches them. I will own my part of that impact, but I cannot live their whole emotional process for them." You can:

Acknowledge: "I know this affects you."

Apologize for what's truly yours: "I'm sorry for the way I handled X."

Clarify: "This is about my capacity, not your worth."

Provide what you reasonably can: "Here's how I can help with the transition." You cannot: Control how they interpret your decision, make them see your heart, force them to bless what they don't understand, stop them from telling their version of the story. That's painful—and also part of being an adult who makes real choices.

When Leadership Requires Moving Cheese. If you're a leader—at work, at church, in your family, in a project—you will sometimes be the one who: Changes direction, reassigns roles, ends programs, enforces boundaries or says "no more" to what everyone was used to. And people will feel it. They may say:

- *"We've always done it this way."*

- *"Why are you changing everything?"*

- *"You don't care about us / the history / the culture."*

- *"The old leader never would've…"*

You might be tempted to: Keep everyone comfortable instead of doing what's right, overexplain until you're emotionally drained, reverse good decisions just to stop the noise. Instead, practice clear, compassionate leadership:

- Explain the "why" as much as is wise and appropriate.

- Name what you know people are losing.

- Create as much support as you realistically can during the change.

- Accept that some will still be upset.

Leadership that never moves anyone's cheese is not leadership; it's management of the status quo.

Sometimes love looks like disruption.

When Your Healing Breaks an Old Agreement. Many relationships—romantic, friendship, family, church—are built on unspoken agreements like:

- "I'll stay small so you can stay comfortable."

- "I'll be the strong one so you don't have to face your own weakness."

- "I'll absorb the blame so you don't have to grow."

- "I'll give you spiritual performance, so you don't have to wrestle with hard questions."

- "I'll always be available, so you never feel abandoned."

When you heal, you start breaking those agreements. You say:

- "I can't carry that for you anymore."

- "I'm not going to lie about how I feel."

- "I'm not going to be your emotional dumping ground."

- "I'm not going to pretend this is healthy."

To the other person, it can feel like betrayal: "You changed the rules." "You're not who I married / met / raised / pastored." "You used to be fine with this." The truth? You were never fine. You were just coping. You are allowed to outgrow agreements that were built on your own self-abandonment. That will move other people's cheese. It still might be the most honest, loving thing you've ever done—for you and, eventually, for them.

How to Communicate Change Without Collapsing. If your decisions are about to shift other people's world, communication matters. You don't owe everyone a TED Talk, but you can aim for:

Clarity

"Here's the change I'm making."

"Here's when it will happen."

"Here's what this means for you in practical terms."

Ownership

"This decision is about my capacity / calling / health."

"I recognize I could have communicated sooner or differently in the past."

Care

"I know this may be disappointing / inconvenient."

"I'm grateful for what we've shared in this role / season."

"Here's how I'd like to end or transition well, if you're open."

Boundaries

"This decision is final."

"I'm open to hearing how you feel, but I may not be able to change the decision."

"I can talk about this for X more time today, then I need to step away."

You cannot guarantee how they'll receive it. You can only steward how you deliver it.

What If You Actually Did Harm? Sometimes, we don't just move people's cheese—we knock it over in the dark. Because we were:

Immature. Avoidant. Unhealed. Careless. Overwhelmed and didn't ask for help. You may look back and realize:

- "I ghosted that community instead of closing things well."
- "I ended that relationship in a way that was cruel or confusing."
- "I overpromised and underdelivered, and people paid for it."
- "I used 'calling' or 'God said' language to avoid owning my part."

What do you do then? Tell the truth to yourself first.

- "I hurt them."
- "I mishandled that."
- "I used my pain as an excuse."

Discern whether direct repair is wise and possible. Is it safe? Are there power dynamics or legal issues to consider? Would reaching out help them—or just make you feel better? Where appropriate, apologize specifically. "I'm sorry I disappeared instead of having a hard conversation." "I'm sorry I minimized your feelings when I made that decision." "I'm sorry I used spiritual language to shut down your questions."

Change your patterns going forward. Repair is not just about words. It's about making different choices next time you're tempted to do the same thing. Owning harm doesn't mean you stay stuck in shame. It means you refuse to pretend you were just "following your peace" when you were actually avoiding responsibility.

Blessing People You Can't Take With You. There will be people you love deeply who simply cannot or will not go where you're going. Not because they're evil. Not because you're better. Because your paths diverge. You may feel pressure to: Drag them along, stay where you are so they're not alone, dim your growth so they don't feel left behind. Instead, you can practice a different posture:

- I can love you from a different distance.

- I can honor what we had without forcing what we don't have anymore.
- I can bless you without betraying myself."

Sometimes that blessing is silent. Sometimes it's spoken:

- "Thank you for who you were to me in that season."
- "I'm grateful for what we shared, even though we're not in the same place now."
- "I wish you well, truly."

When you start to see yourself as "someone whose choices move other people's cheese," two equal and opposite lies show up. One says, "If you were truly loving/spiritual/mature, you'd find a way to grow without inconveniencing anyone." The other says, "If they don't like it, that's their problem, full stop."

Neither is true. You are not a demolition crew sent to wreck other people's lives. You are also not a piece of furniture they get to arrange indefinitely. You are a person whose life will, inevitably, rearrange other people's furniture. The point of this chapter is not to make you terrified of taking up space. It's to train you to notice the impact of your movement and respond like an adult, not a ghost or a bulldozer.

The Myth of the Painless Upgrade. There's a fantasy version of growth where everyone claps. You get healthier, and the people who benefitted from your unhealth say, "We're so proud of you."

You set boundaries, and the people who were used to your 24/7 availability say, "Thank you for modeling self-care." You leave a role, and the people who depended on you immediately find their footing and send you fruit baskets. Sometimes, pieces of that do happen. But usually, growth looks less like a Hallmark movie and more like an awkward family group chat.

"Well, I guess we know who you care about now."

"Wow. Must be nice to just do what you want."

"So I guess all that talk about commitment meant nothing."

You're over here trying to save your mental health, and someone is acting like you just set fire to the village. It's tempting, in that moment, to either:

Abort the upgrade ("Never mind, I'll just stay miserable"), or

Emotionally flip the table ("Fine, I don't owe anyone anything").

What you actually owe is this: to tell yourself the truth about what's happening. You're not choosing between "growth with zero impact" and "growth that makes you a villain."

You're choosing between:

Growing with awareness (I see how this will affect you),

Growing with honesty (I'm not going to pretend this is cost-free), and

Growing with courage (I'm still going to move, because the alternative is self-erasure).

The upgrade was never going to be painless. The question is whether you turn the pain into a story about your selfishness—or into a doorway to more honest relationships.

Are You Leaving a Role or a Throne? Sometimes when you "step down," you're not just leaving a job or a ministry or a family role. You're vacating a throne. Not because you asked for one. Sometimes it just… formed around you. You became:

The unofficial therapist of the group.

The one who always picked up the slack at work.

The glue of the friend circle.

The spiritual answer machine.

The family crisis-manager.

People started organizing themselves around your reliability. So when you say, "I can't do this anymore," they're not just losing help. They're losing a stabilizing myth: *"As long as you're here, we don't have to change."*

When that myth dies, people grieve. Some grieve by crying. Some by withdrawing. Some by fighting you. Some by suddenly finding "theological reasons" why your decision is wrong. It's disorienting to realize, "Oh, I wasn't just doing a job. I was holding up an entire emotional economy." You don't fix that by climbing back onto the throne. You also don't fix it by pretending the throne never existed.

You tell the simple, un-royal truth:

"I am a person who did what I could for a while. I can't do it in this way anymore. I trust that, over time, you will find other ways to get what you need that don't require me to disappear."

You may have to repeat that to yourself more than to them. Because part of you is used to the throne, too. Part of you liked being the one they couldn't imagine functioning without. That's not evil. It's just honest data. Stepping down means losing that, as well. You are not only giving up burden; you're giving up a certain kind of importance. Letting yourself grieve that without crawling back up is a quiet, underrated courage.

When Your Boundary Sounds Like an Insult (But Isn't). Few sentences cause more drama than: "I can't keep doing that. "You think you're talking about your schedule, your nervous system, your bandwidth. They hear: "You're not worth it." You say, "I can't answer calls after 10 p.m. anymore." They hear, "You're too much." You say, "I'm not available to serve every week." They hear, "You don't matter to me." You say, "I need to step back from being the one who plans everything." They hear, "You're a burden."

This translation problem is not entirely your fault. Many of us were trained—by family patterns, church cultures, workplaces—that love = unlimited access. So any limit, however reasonable, feels like rejection. You cannot rewire all those associations for someone else. You can refuse to play along with the false equation. Instead of debating their feelings ("You shouldn't feel abandoned"), stick to two tracks:

State the boundary cleanly.

"I'm not able to do X past Y time." "I can't keep leading this after Z date."

Name what it is—and is not—about.

"This is about my health, not your value." "This is about my capacity, not about whether I care."

They may not believe you at first. That doesn't automatically mean you're wrong. It may mean that this is the first time they've met someone who refuses to prove love by self-destruction. Over time, people who are willing to grow will start to see, "Oh. You really did stay. You just stopped doing the parts that required you to disappear." People who are not willing to grow will keep insisting that any limit is an insult. You will be tempted to take that on as your fault. *It isn't.* Their feelings are real. Their interpretation is not law.

You Don't Have to Send a Memo to Everyone. One of the exhausting parts of moving other people's cheese is the feeling that you owe the entire world a press conference. You are not a public company. You are a person. Not everyone needs: A full backstory, A theological justification, A detailed health report, or A ten-point vision statement for your next season. Some people do deserve more context: spouses, kids, close friends, people directly affected at work or ministry.

Others are not stakeholders in your actual life. They are spectators. Spectators will often demand the same access as stakeholders. "Why weren't we consulted?" "Why didn't you tell us earlier?" "How could you do this without checking with us?" The honest answer, which you should say internally even if you don't say it out loud, is: *"Because this is not actually your decision."*

You can be polite without being porous. You might say: *I appreciate your concern. This is something I've processed with the people directly involved, and the decision is made.* If they push for more, remember: curiosity is not a claim. People can be as curious as they want about your life. That doesn't obligate you to hand them the microphone. One of the ways you know you're growing is when you stop giving long explanations to people who are only asking so they can have an opinion, not so they can share a burden.

The "You Changed" Accusation. There's a special tone people use when they say, "You've changed." They rarely mean, "You've become more patient and emotionally literate, congratulations." They mean, "You are no longer playing the role I wrote for you, and I don't like this new script."

In some communities, "you changed" is the worst thing they can think to say. It's almost a theological accusation.

"You used to be so on fire."

"You used to be so available."

"You used to say yes to everything."

"You used to be humble."

Translation: "You used to be more convenient for me." There are two questions worth asking yourself when you hear, "You changed." *Is it true?* Often, yes. You did change. You went to therapy. You started sleeping. You stopped volunteering for every crisis. You stopped agreeing with things that made your stomach hurt. Is it bad? That's the real question. "I'm less codependent than I used to be" is a change. "I'm less manipulable by guilt than I used to be" is a change. "I have fewer panic attacks because I'm not living at everyone's beck and call" is a change.

If someone is using "you changed" as a synonym for "you betrayed us," check whose "us" they're talking about. *If "us" = "the version of us that only works if you stay unhealed,"* then yes, you betrayed that. *Good.* You are not obligated to stay sick so other people don't have to see a doctor.

When Saying "No" Reveals the Real Relationship. One of the uncomfortable side effects of moving other people's cheese is that you discover what the relationship was actually built on.

You thought:

"This friendship is about mutual care."

"This ministry team is about shared calling."

"This job is about my skills and contribution."

"This family bond is about love."

Then you change one variable—say no, step back, move away, shift a pattern—and suddenly the vibe changes.

The friend goes silent.

The church stops calling.

The job treats you as replaceable.

The family member launches a character assassination tour.

It's disorienting. You realize, "Oh. This wasn't primarily about me as a person. It was about the function I performed." That hurts. It's also clarifying. You're not wrong for feeling grief or anger. You're also not wrong for refusing to go back to a version of the relationship that required you to be a function instead of a person. Sometimes the most honest thing you can say to yourself is:

"I loved them. They loved what I did for them. Those are not the same thing." It doesn't mean there was no genuine affection. It means the affection was entangled with dependence in a way that couldn't survive your growth. *That's tragic.* It's also a sign you're outgrowing transactional love. You will, if you keep going, find people who still love you when you're not fixing their life. They'll be the ones who don't punish you for getting better.

The Temptation to Over-Correct. If you've spent years over-giving, over-functioning, and over-owning, your first attempts at change may swing too far the other way.

You stop answering any calls.

You bail without any explanation.

You decline everything because "I'm protecting my peace."

You justify every withdrawal with "God told me," even when what God actually said was, "Maybe talk to a human being."

This is understandable.

When you've been on one extreme for a long time, the middle feels invisible. But if you're not careful, you'll start doing the very things to others that once hurt you:

Disappearing without closure.

Using vague spiritual language to dodge responsibility.

Acting like anyone who's disappointed by your decision is "toxic."

Not everyone who is hurt by your change is manipulative.

Some are just… hurt. They liked serving with you. They loved working with you. They had plans that included you.

A clean "no" doesn't require you to call them idolaters for being sad. There's a difference between:

"I can't keep doing this, and I understand that's painful," and

"I can't keep doing this, and if you feel anything about it, that proves you're unhealthy."

You don't have to weaponize your growth. You can let it be what it is: a necessary adjustment that will, yes, frustrate some people—and that's okay. You are allowed to learn balance in real time, imperfectly, with some apologies along the way.

The Quiet Courage of Staying in the Conversation (Until It's Time Not To). When your decision hurts or scares someone, their first reaction might be messy. They might say things they don't mean.

They might drag up old history. They might question your motives, your character, your faith, your loyalty, your sanity. You do not have to stay for abuse. But you also don't have to flee at the first sign of discomfort. Sometimes the most healing thing you can do—for them and for you—is to stay in the conversation just long enough to let the first wave pass.

To say, "I hear that you're angry. I'm not going to defend myself right now. I just want to be clear about what's changing and what's not."

To say, "I get that this feels sudden to you. In my head and body, it's been building for a long time. I should have said something sooner. I'm saying it now."

To say, "We might not agree about this. I still care about you."

Staying present like that is not the same as reopening the negotiation about your decision. It's about giving the relationship a chance to absorb the impact without everything shattering on first contact. Then—and this is important— you leave the room, metaphorically or literally, when your part is done. You don't stay indefinitely trying to manage their every feeling. You don't keep explaining in the hope of getting unanimous approval.

You give what you can: a clear word, an honest heart, a soft tone. And then you let their process belong to them. The courage is in both directions: staying long enough to be real, leaving soon enough to be free.

When You're the "Villain" in Someone Else's Testimony. At some point, you will hear a version of your story where you're the bad guy. In a small group. On a podcast. In a book. At a dinner you're not invited to.

You'll be the one who "walked away," "changed," "stopped serving," "got proud," "hurt the ministry," "abandoned the family," "chose career over call- ing." You will want, deeply, to correct the record. Sometimes you should. If the story is doing real harm to your reputation or work, or if lies are being used to control others, there's a place for saying, "That's not what happened," with specifics.

But often, the story is not about factual accuracy. It's about how that per- son experienced your change. You may be 80% sure you did the right thing, in the right way, for the right reasons. They may be 100% sure you ruined their life. Both perceptions can exist in the same universe without one of you being a cartoon villain. It helps to remember: You are the hero in your own narrative, but a side character in theirs. Their story will emphasize what your decision cost them, not what it saved you. They are allowed to grieve their losses, even if those losses came from your healthy "yes."

You don't have to accept every accusation as truth. You also don't have to chase every room where your name comes up. Sometimes the most radical act of trust is to let God, time, and your consistent character do more for your reputation than any counter-testimony ever could. You keep living in a way that, over years, makes it harder and harder for the "villain" version of you to stick.

Not because you're perfect. Because you're not hiding.

Letting Other People Find Their Own Cheese. Here's a strange side effect of moving someone else's cheese with integrity: you may actually be giving them a chance to find a cheese that is theirs, not yours.

As long as you:

Always said yes,

Always solved the problem,

Always filled the gap,

Always carried emotional weight,

They never had to find out:

What they're capable of,

What they actually want,

What they believe when you're not feeding them lines,

Who else in their life can show up.

Your exit, your boundary, your "no," might be the first time they:

Pick up responsibility they'd been avoiding,

Ask for help from someone else,

Realize they'd made you their source instead of God, or instead of doing their own work.

It may take a long time for them to see that.

You might never get to witness it. But it happens more often than you think. A parent who stops being the 24/7 financial safety net sometimes discovers, years later, that their adult child finally learned to budget. A pastor who steps down from being the only counselor sometimes hears that people started going to therapy—and actually got better. A friend who stops being the constant rescuer occasionally gets a message out of the blue: "I was mad at you then. Now I see why you stepped back. It forced me to grow."

You can't time this. You can't guarantee it. You can only act in such a way that, if they do eventually grow, your conscience is clear: you moved their cheese with as much truth and kindness as you had, even when they hated it. The rest is not up to you. You will move people's cheese simply by being alive, honest, and in motion.

Sometimes your decisions will feel like betrayal to people who preferred you smaller. Sometimes your boundaries will sound like rejection to people who equate love with exhaustion. Sometimes your healing will be the most disruptive thing that's ever happened to a system built on your unhealed self. You are not called to be reckless with that power. You are also not called to bury it. The invitation is to become the kind of person who can say, with a straight face and a soft heart:

> *"My life will rearrange other people's plans. That's unavoidable. I will do my best to move through this world in a way that is honest, kind, and clear. I will own what's mine, release what's not, and keep growing anyway."*

That won't make you universally liked. But it will make you real. And real people, in the end, are the only ones who can love, lead, and leave well when the cheese has to move.

When "You're Hurting Us" Is Really "Don't Move". Not every "you're hurting us" is abuse or manipulation. Sometimes it's just honest pain. But sometimes, it's code for, "We liked it better when you didn't have needs." You'll know it's the second one when:

The person only brings up "unity" or "love" when you're about to change something. They were fine with your exhaustion, but furious about your boundary. Their concern for your "calling" always seems to involve you doing more for them, not less.

"You're abandoning us."

"You're breaking covenant."

"You're disrupting what God is doing here."

"You're destroying the culture."

Those are heavy accusations. They land on the softest, most sincere parts of you. The parts that genuinely don't want to cause harm. The parts that have given, and given, and given. If you're not careful, you'll hear: *"You're hurting us," and translate it as, "You must be wrong."*

There's a question worth asking in those moments: "If I stayed exactly as I am—same availability, same work, same lack of sleep—would they still be saying I'm hurting them? "If the answer is no, then what you're hearing isn't a moral evaluation. *It's withdrawal symptoms.* They are going through detox from a version of you that was always on-call.

Detox hurts. But the pain of detox doesn't prove the drug was healthy. Sometimes the loudest "You're hurting us" is actually "We don't want to feel what our own growth would require." You can care about their pain without letting it chain you to who you used to be.

The Economics of Your Yes. Every yes you've given has a budget.

Time.

Energy.

Money.

Attention.

Health.

Invisible labor.

Someone has been paying for your generosity.

Sometimes it's you—your sleep, your hobbies, your body.

Sometimes it's your spouse who picked up 90% of the home load.

Sometimes it's your kids who got the leftovers of your patience.

Sometimes it's the quiet friend who never asks you for anything because they know you're always wrung out from everyone else.

On the outside, people saw: "You're so committed.", "You're always there.", "You never say no.", On the inside, your life had a spreadsheet that never balanced. When you move someone else's cheese by stepping back, you're not suddenly becoming selfish. You're finally doing the math out loud.

"I can't keep funding this with my nervous system."

"I can't keep subsidizing this ministry with my marriage."

"I can't keep paying for this job with my health."

Most systems are quite happy for you to overspend, as long as the results look good. They rarely come to you and say, "We've noticed you're burning your life at both ends. Please stop." They say, "We're so grateful. You're such a blessing."

So when you finally re-do the budget—when you say no, or less, or "not like this"—it can feel like betrayal to people who got used to cheap labor. From their perspective, the cost of your yes just went up. From your perspective, the cost was always there. You're just refusing to hide the invoice in your body anymore. This is not greed. It's stewardship. You are the one person who has to live inside your life full-time. You get a vote in how it's spent.

Different Roles, Different Reactions. When you move your cheese, not everyone is affected in the same way. Kids, congregants, staff, peers, parents, friends—they have different vantage points and different losses. Expecting them to respond the same way will make you crazy.

Kids. Kids don't care about your "strategic transition" language. They care about:

"Are you still coming to my game?"

"Are we moving?"

"Does this mean you're more stressed or less?"

They will often react with:
Clinginess ("Don't go to that meeting.")

Acting out in unrelated areas.

Asking the same question 47 times.

This is not a referendum on your decision. It's their way of asking, "Are we still safe in this?"

You don't need to give them all the adult details. You do need to make eye contact and say some version of:

"Here's what this means for you," not just, *"Here's what this means for my calling."*

Congregants / Community Members. If you're a pastor or leader in a faith space, your move will hit people in complicated ways.

You've:

Married them.

Buried their loved ones.

Sat in their hospital rooms.

Heard their confessions.

You are not just "staff." You are a symbol of continuity, comfort, and God's presence (fairly or unfairly).

So when you leave or change roles, some people will experience it as:

Spiritual abandonment.

Proof that "everyone leaves."

A threat to their fragile trust in God. You cannot fix all of that.

You can name it. You can say, "I know this may stir up old losses for some of you. I can't stop that from happening. I can tell you: my leaving this role is not God leaving you." You are changing jobs. In their hearts, it feels like the ground is moving. Honoring that doesn't mean staying. It means not trivializing what you mean to them.

Staff / Team. Your team's reactions will often be more pragmatic and more political. They're thinking:

"What happens to my job?"

"Who will be in charge?"

"Is this promotion or chaos?"

"Do I have a future here without you?"

Some will be sad. Some will be secretly relieved. Some will see opportunity. Some will update their résumés before your announcement ends. *That mix is normal.* You're not their parent or their messiah. You are a key variable in their professional life. When you change, they have to re-run their own calculations. The most honoring thing you can do is:

Be as clear as you can about timelines.

Refuse to make promises you can't keep.

Avoid using them as your emotional support group about your decision.

They deserve your clarity. They do not exist to manage your ambivalence.

Peers / Friends. Peers often have the strangest reactions.

Some will be genuinely thrilled.

Some will be supportive in public and low-key threatened in private.

Some will distance themselves because your change is shining a light on their own stuckness.

If you step out of a burning-out lifestyle, the friend who's still in one has choices: Be inspired.

Be challenged. Be resentful. You don't get to pick which they choose.

You do get to notice which ones can celebrate you when your life stops matching theirs. Those are the ones you can probably carry into your next season. The rest? You can still love them. Just don't use their reactions as a verdict on whether you were allowed to move.

Five Years Later: The Long View of Your "Selfish" Decision. In the moment, your decision will feel huge. Earth-shattering. Unforgivable. Irreversible.

Then time passes.

The church that swore it would collapse without you… doesn't.

The team that couldn't imagine functioning without you… figures it out.

The friend who said you were abandoning them… finds new support.

The family member who accused you of ruining everything… adapts more than they expected.

Five years out, the story often looks very different than it did in the first six months.

You might see:

People flourishing in roles they only discovered because you left.

New leaders rising who never would've had a chance under the old setup.

Your kids calmer because home stopped being an extension of your overwork.

Your own body finally not living in permanent emergency mode.

You may also see: Some relationships that never recovered. A few people who still tell the "villain" version of your decision. Opportunities you genuinely lost by stepping away. Both sets of outcomes are real. But here's what's almost always true:

The thing that felt like the end of the world for some people was actually the end of a pattern.

Patterns end loudly. The first time you say, "No," after a decade of "Yes," it causes more noise than the previous hundred yeses. But five years later, most people aren't replaying your one big "no" in their heads. They're living the lives that grew up around it. You don't get to control those lives. You do get to ask, looking back, "Would I rather be living with the consequences of that decision—or of never making it?"

Most people, even with scars, answer, "I'm glad I moved."

The PR Department in Your Head. You may never hire an actual publicist. But almost all of us have an internal PR department that spins our decisions. It writes imaginary statements:

"After much prayer and consideration…"

"Due to circumstances beyond my control…"

"In this season, I feel led…"

It scripts how you'll explain yourself at reunions, on social media, in Christmas letters. It rehearses the conversation where your biggest critic finally understands and says, "Wow, I misjudged you. You were right all along." Here's the uncomfortable truth: Most of those fantasy conversations will never happen. The person you're "explaining yourself to in the shower" may never give you a hearing in real life. The crowd you're trying to pre-emptively convince may not even be thinking about you. If you're not careful, you'll spend more energy managing your imaginary reputation than living your actual life. There's a question that can calm the PR department down:

> *"If nobody ever fully understands this decision but me and God, would it still be the right one?"*

If the answer is no, maybe you need more clarity. If the answer is yes, your job is to act—then accept that some people will never get the memo. You can still communicate well. You can still do your best to be clear and kind. But at some point, the spokesperson in your head has to sit down so the rest of you can move on. You're not running a brand campaign. You're trying to be a human being who tells the truth with your life.

You do not have to demonize someone to release them.

CHEESE CHECK

This final chapter is about becoming more aware and more honest about the ways your choices move other people's cheese—and walking in that with integrity.

Whose cheese has your recent growth or decisions moved the most?

Name 2–3 people or groups (family, team, church, partner, friends).

What changed for them because of your decision?

Where are you feeling misplaced guilt vs. healthy guilt?

Misplaced: "I feel bad just for having needs / limits / dreams."

Healthy: "I feel convicted about how I handled something."

Write one sentence for each.

Is there one place you need to communicate a change more clearly?

Who needs to hear it?

What's one sentence you could say to begin?

"I haven't said this directly yet, but I need to let you know that _________."

Is there any repair you sense you should attempt?

If yes, what would a simple, specific apology sound like?

If no (not safe / not wise), how can you honor that situation by changing your future patterns?

Where do you need to release over-responsibility for someone else's emotional journey?

Complete: "I can care about how _________ feels, but I cannot carry _________ for them."

Write a short blessing for the people whose cheese your obedience or growth has moved.

For example:

May those affected by my decisions find their own path, support, and peace.

May they discover new provision where I am no longer their source.

May my growth never be their ruin—and may their story with God and themselves continue beyond me."

You will move people's cheese just by being a person who changes, grows, obeys God, and honors your limits. The invitation is not to stop changing. It's to change cleanly—with as much truth, kindness, and courage as you can.

CHEESE CHECK NOTES

You learn to live with your new cheese

instead of mentally camping in the old maze.

Dr. Laide R. Alexander

Walking the Maze
With Your Eyes Open

You've walked through a lot of rooms in this book. We've named the many ways cheese moves:

- Life moves it without asking you.

- You move it to survive.

- You move it to grow.

- You move it to hide.

- You don't move it at all—you let others move it for you.

- You move it on purpose, with a clear why.

- You learn to live with your new cheese instead of mentally camping in the old maze.

- Your moves shake your relationships.

Your shifting roles force you to ask, *Who am I without that cheese?* The cheese moves again, and you face change with less self-condemnation. And finally, you see that sometimes you are the one moving the cheese for others. Underneath all of this, three truths have been quietly repeating: You are allowed to change. You are responsible for how you change. You are more than any maze you've ever walked.

This Was Never Just About the Cheese. The jobs, roles, churches, cities, relationships, titles, and assignments—all of that matters. **They shape you. They feed you. They stretch you.**

But they do not define you.

What this journey has really been about is: Your patterns. Your honesty. Your boundaries. Your courage. Your faith. Your agency. Your healing. It's about learning to ask, before you move:

- "What's my real why?"

- "What part of this is about me?"

- "What will this cost, and am I willing to pay it?"

- "Am I running from something—or toward something?"

And after you move:

- "How do I live here fully, not halfway?"

- "What new rhythms does this season require?"

- "How do I honor what was without getting stuck there?"

- "How do I tell the truth about my story—without making myself the hero or the victim in every scene?"

You Are Not Powerless in This Maze. Yes, life will keep moving. Yes, some things will happen without your consent. Yes, there will be losses you did not choose and would never have chosen. But even there, you are not just: A character in other people's decisions. A victim of circumstances. A prop in someone else's calling. You have: A voice. A will. A mind. A story. A God (if that's your faith) who sees more than the one hallway you're in right now. You may not always get to choose what happens. But you always get to choose how you will respond, who you will become, and whether you will tell yourself the truth. That is not small. That is your power.

You Don't Have to Move Alone. If there is a thread you can carry out of these pages, let it be this: Wherever the cheese moves next, you don't have to navigate it alone, and you don't have to disappear to survive it. Lean into:

- Wise friends and mentors

- Therapy or counseling, if available

- Healthy spiritual community

- Practices that anchor your body, heart, and hope

Your own growing ability to discern, decide, and communicate. And as you keep walking, keep asking gentle, honest questions of yourself:

- "Am I abandoning myself here—or honoring myself?"

- "Am I repeating an old pattern—or writing a new page?"

- "What would the wiser, older version of me thank me for doing right now?"

You've just spent an entire book paying attention to something most people only notice when it blows up their life. You've named moves you chose and moves you never would have. Rooms you outgrew and rooms that shrank around you. Seasons where you ran toward something and seasons where, if you're honest, you were mostly running away. You've looked at the ways your shifting has shaken other people. You've seen how often you tried to hold still so nobody else had to feel it.

That's not nothing.

Most people never pause long enough to see their own pattern, let alone question it. You did. So if you feel a little tender, a little exposed, a little "now what?"—that's appropriate. You've been walking around the maze with the lights on. This is where a lot of stories would try to reassure you that from here on out, everything will be smooth. You know better. ***The cheese will move again.***

Jobs will end.

Bodies will change.

Kids will grow.

Churches will shift.

Leaders will come and go.

Your own desires will surprise you.

There will be moments when you can barely remember why you said yes to this chapter, or why you ever thought you could survive the last one. When that happens, don't go hunting for a perfect formula in these pages. Go looking for the version of you that started telling the truth.

The you who finally admitted, "This isn't working."

The you who dared to say, "I need help."

The you who whispered, "I can't keep living like this," and didn't stuff it back down this time.

That person is still in there. You don't need a brand-new self for every hallway. You need a steadily truer one. You may still not know exactly "who you are" without that role, that church, that relationship, that title. That's okay.

Identity is not a single cheese you find once and protect at all costs. It's something you grow into, piece by honest piece, every time you:

Tell the truth a little sooner than you used to.

Choose rest a little earlier than you used to.

Stay present a little longer than you used to.

Say no a little cleaner than you used to.

Ask for help a little braver than you used to.

Those are small moves. They don't trend. They don't get standing ovations. But they quietly change the kind of person walking the maze. And that, in the end, is the point. Not that you never get lost. Not that you always choose the "right" door on the first try. But that, over time, you become someone who is less easy to bully, less easy to flatter, less easy to guilt, less easy to knock out of yourself. Someone who can sit in a hallway between cheeses and say, "This is not the end of me. This is just a hallway. "As you close this book, nothing magical happens.

Your inbox is still full.

The hard conversation is still waiting.

The decision you've been postponing didn't resolve itself while you were reading.

But you are not the same person who opened to page one.

You have language now for things you used to only feel.

You have categories for choices you used to blur together.

You have questions you can ask when everything in you wants to shut down or sprint.

You have, whether you feel it or not, a little more holy suspicion of the lies that kept you stuck.

You are allowed to take that seriously. You are allowed to act on it.

Not dramatically. Not all at once. Maybe it looks like one honest conversation you've been avoiding. One small boundary you hold this week. One application you finally submit. One "I'm not okay" you say out loud to a safe person. One "thank you and goodbye" you stop rewriting and actually send.

Tiny moves. Real ones. This book can't walk those steps for you. But it can sit in your bag or on your shelf as a quiet witness that you once decided your life was worth examining—and that you could, if you chose, decide that again tomorrow. So as the maze keeps shifting, here's the invitation:

- Don't waste energy pretending nothing is moving.
- Don't waste years pretending you have no say.
- Let what you've seen here make you more awake, not more afraid.
- More honest, not more hardened.

More thoughtful about your impact, not more paralyzed by it. And when the next move comes—and it will—may you remember, even for a moment:

- You've been here before.
- You have language now.
- You have choices now.
- You have people or can find them.
- You have a God who is not surprised by a single hallway.

You do not have to like every season. You do not have to enjoy every move.

You are simply invited to stay present for your own life as it unfolds—to keep showing up in the story as yourself, not just as the role other people assigned you. If all this book does is make you a little less likely to abandon yourself the next time the floor shifts, it will have done something holy.

You don't owe the maze perfection. You owe it your presence.

Go live the next chapter with as much truth as you have today. When you run out, ask for more. And when the cheese moves again, as it surely will, may you recognize the sound—not as proof that you're cursed or behind, but as another chance to practice what you already know:

You are allowed to change.

You are responsible for how you change.

You are, and always have been, more than any maze you'll ever walk.

A Final Blessing for Your Next Moves

As you close this chapter and step back into your real, messy, beautiful life, receive this as a kind of benediction:

May you have the courage to leave what is killing you, and the patience to stay where you're meant to grow.

May you have the wisdom to tell the truth about your patterns, without drowning in shame.

May you have the strength to set boundaries that honor your soul, even when others don't understand.

May you remember that titles, roles, and rooms will change, but your worth does not.

May you be surrounded by a few people who can handle your evolution, not just your performance.

My you learn to bless the seasons and people that fed you for a time, even as you release what can't go with you. And when the cheese moves again—as it surely will— may you find yourself a little more anchored, a little more honest, a little more whole than the last time it did. You don't have to master the maze. You just have to keep walking it with open eyes, an open heart, and a growing refusal to live any chapter of your life without you in it.

Why Move My Cheese?
Practice Guide

A 6-Session Journey for Individuals, Teams, and Faith Communities

U se this guide on your own, with a friend, with your team, or with your church/small group. Each session is built around the same simple rhythm: Read —Reflect —Name —Decide —Share.

How It's Structured

6 sessions (can be 6 weeks, 6 meetings, or done at your own pace)

Each session links to 1–2 chapters, but the questions stand alone

Every session has:

Focus (what this session is about)

Key Chapters (for those who want to read/review first)

Core Questions for individuals

Group/Team Prompts (optional)

One Small Move (a concrete action before the next session)

Session 1

Naming Your Current Cheese Move

Focus: Get clear on what's actually changing right now—and how much of it you chose.

Key Chapters:

1 —When Change Happens to You
2 —The Question Behind the Question

Core Questions (Individual):

What is the biggest "cheese move" in my life right now?

Job, relationship, church, health, city, role, identity?

How much of this change was:

Chosen by me?

Chosen by others?

Forced by circumstances?

Where am I most tempted to ask, "Who did this to me?"

Where might I need to add, "What will I do now—and why?"

Group/Team Prompts:

Invite each person (or department) to answer:

"Right now, what's shifting for me/us is ___________."

As an organization: name 2–3 major changes in the last 12–18 months.

Ask: "Which of these were reactive? Which were intentional?"

One Small Move:

Write one honest sentence starting with:

"Right now, I am in a season of ___________."

Post it somewhere you'll see it this week.

Session 2
Survival, Growth, or Hiding?

Focus: Discern the real motive behind recent or upcoming moves.

Key Chapters:

3 —I Moved My Cheese to Survive

4 —I Moved My Cheese to Grow

5 —I Moved My Cheese to Hide

Core Questions (Individual):

Think of one big move (past or present). Which best fits:

Survival

Growth

Hiding

Why?

Where have I called something "growth" that was really "escape"?

Where have I called something "selfish" that was actually survival?

What patterns do I notice in my past moves?

(Do I mostly move to avoid pain, to chase opportunity, or to disappear?)

Group/Team Prompts:

As a team, label a few past decisions:

"We moved to survive when…"

"We moved to grow when…"

"We moved to hide when…"

Ask: "What do we want our next major move to be primarily about?"

One Small Move:

Complete this sentence in writing:

"The next time I feel the urge to move, I will pause long enough to ask, 'Is this survival, growth, or hiding?'"

Session 3
Agency and Boundaries

Focus: Shift from letting others move your cheese to owning your part—and your limits.

Key Chapters:

6 —I Let Other People Move My Cheese

7 —Moving Your Cheese on Purpose

Core Questions (Individual):

Where have I quietly handed other people the power to decide for me?

("I'll just go along," "Whatever you think," "I guess I have no choice.")

What are 1–2 unspoken rules I've lived by (family, culture, church, workplace) that have kept me from saying no or choosing differently?

Where do I need one clearer boundary right now—at work, at church, at home?

Group/Team Prompts:

As a group, discuss: "Where do we tend to let outside pressure make decisions for us (social media, tradition, donors, 'we've always done it this way')?"

Identify one area where the team/organization needs a clearer boundary (scope, hours, priorities, who we are not).

One Small Move:

Write one boundary sentence and practice saying it out loud:

"For this season, I am not available for __________."

or

"As a team, we will no longer say yes to __________."

Session 4
Living With New Cheese (Instead of Camping in the Old Maze)

Focus: Stop mentally living in the past; build rhythms that match where you actually are.

Key Chapters:

8 —Living With Your New Cheese
10 —Who Am I Without That Cheese?

Core Questions (Individual):

Where am I physically in a new season but mentally still in the old one?
(Still arguing with old bosses, reliving old church conflicts, idealizing an old life.)

What grief have I not given myself permission to feel about what I left?

What does this current season actually require from me in terms of:

Rest

Work

Relationships

Spiritual life / inner life

Group/Team Prompts:

Ask: "What are we still doing 'because we've always done it this way'—even though our current reality has changed?"

Invite each person to name: "One thing from the old season we need to honor and release, and one practice we need to build for this season."

One Small Move:

Choose one tiny rhythm that matches your current season (not your ideal one):

10-minute daily walk

Weekly planning time

A standing 30-minute team check-in

Commit to trying it for 7 days.

Session 5
Relationships and Impact

Focus: Face how your moves affect others—who comes with you, who doesn't, and how to communicate.

Key Chapters:

9 —When Your Cheese Move Shakes Your Relationships

12 —When You're the One Moving Someone Else's Cheese

Core Questions (Individual):

Whose cheese did my last major decision move (family, friends, coworkers, church, clients)?

Where am I carrying misplaced guilt (feeling bad just for having needs/limits), and where do I feel healthy conviction (I mishandled something)?

Is there:

A conversation I need to have?

An apology I need to offer?

A weight I need to stop carrying for someone else?

Group/Team Prompts:

Map stakeholders: "Who is most impacted by our recent or upcoming changes?"

For each group, ask:

"What do they lose?"

"What can we communicate or offer to support them (within our limits)?"

One Small Move:

Write one sentence you need to say to someone:

"I haven't said this directly yet, but I need to let you know that ___________."

Decide: Will you say it? When and how?

Session 6
Your Change Profile and Next Moves

Focus: Name your patterns with change, build anchors, and choose how you want to move from here.

Key Chapters:

11 —When the Cheese Moves Again

Conclusion
Walking the Maze With Your Eyes Open

Core Questions (Individual):

When change hits, I tend to:

Rush into the next thing

Freeze and avoid decisions

Over-research and never decide

Hand the decision to someone else

Where have I seen this before?

What are my body anchors, heart anchors, and hope anchors for the next 3 months?

Body: __________

Heart: __________

Hope: __________

If the cheese moved again tomorrow, what is one way I'd like to respond differently than last time?

Group/Team Prompts:

As a team, ask: "What is our organizational change profile?"
(Impulsive? Over-cautious? Conflict-avoidant? Over-spiritualizing?)

Name one commitment:

"Next time we face a major decision, we will __________."

One Small Move:

Write a short "change statement" you can return to:

"When the cheese moves again, I will aim to be more ___________ and less ___________, and I will remember that I am allowed to ___________."

Keep it somewhere visible.

Opening Page Text (How to Use This Guide)

You could introduce the whole section with something like:

How to Use This Practice Guide

This guide is for anyone walking through change—individuals, teams, or faith communities. If you're reading alone: Use one session per week. Grab a journal, read the suggested chapters, then work through the Core Questions and choose your One Small Move.

If you're in a small group or team: Set aside 60–90 minutes per session. Ask everyone to read the key chapters beforehand (or read key excerpts aloud), then discuss the Group/Team Prompts and end by naming one concrete next step.

You don't have to do this perfectly. The point is not to "master the maze," but to walk it with more honesty, clarity, and courage than you had last time.

FINALLY
Why Move My Cheese?

Life has a way of rearranging what you thought you could count on.

Jobs end. Relationships shift. Churches change. Your body, your calling, your beliefs evolve. One day you look up and realize: the cheese is not where you left it.

We know how to ask, *"Who moved my cheese?"*

We're less practiced at asking, *"When am I the one moving it—and why?"*

In this honest, compassionate, and practical book, Dr. A. invites you into a deeper conversation about change. Yes, that's what the book is, *"a conversation"*.

Each short chapter ends with a "Cheese Check"—simple, piercing questions that help you connect the book to your real life. You won't find formulas or guarantees here. You will find language, frameworks, and courage for the decisions you already feel stirring.

If you're:

On the edge of a move and wondering, "Am I allowed to do this?"

Sitting in the aftermath of a decision, asking, "Did I do this for the right reasons?"

Tired of feeling like life just happens to you while you quietly disappear … this book is for you.

You are not just a victim of change. You are an agent in your own story.

You may not control every twist in the maze, but you can learn to say—with clarity, humility, and honesty:

"I moved my cheese, and here's why."